Ludwig Wittgenstein

Titles in the series Critical Lives present the work of leading cultural figures of the modern period. Each book explores the life of the artist, writer, philosopher or architect in question and relates it to their major works.

In the same series

Jean Genet
Stephen Barber

James Joyce
Andrew Gibson

Michel Foucault
David Macey

Frank Lloyd Wright
Robert McCarter

Pablo Picasso
Mary Ann Caws

Jean-Paul Sartre
Andrew Leak

Franz Kafka
Sander L. Gilman

Noam Chomsky
Wolfgang B. Sperlich

Guy Debord
Andy Merrifield

Jorge Luis Borges
Jason Wilson

Marcel Duchamp
Caroline Cros

Ludwig Wittgenstein

Edward Kanterian

REAKTION BOOKS

Dedicated to the memory of Onnig Kanterian and Vlad Clisevici

Published by Reaktion Books Ltd
33 Great Sutton Street
London EC1V ODX, UK

www.reaktionbooks.co.uk

First published 2007

Printed and bound in Great Britain
by Cromwell Press Ltd, Trowbridge, Wiltshire

British Library Cataloguing in Publication Data
Kanterian, Edward
    Ludwig Wittgenstein. – (Critical lives)
    1. Wittgenstein, Ludwig, 1889–1951
    I.Title
    192

ISBN-13: 978 1 86189 320 8
ISBN-10: 1 86189 320 5

Contents

Wittgenstein in the 1940s, photographed by his friend Ben Richards in Swansea.

Introduction

Martin Heidegger once started a lecture on Aristotle with the words 'Aristotle was born, worked, and died. Now let us turn to his ideas.' He was implying that any biographical details in the life of a great philosopher are simply irrelevant to his philosophy. All one needs to do in order to understand a philosopher is to study his works, his theses, theories and arguments. An opposing attitude, no less radical, is to view the biography of a thinker as the ultimate key to his work. Every aspect of his personality, any event in his life, any pronouncement on a seemingly unrelated issue, be it art, politics, morals or sex, is secretly connected to his key ideas, and whoever wishes to understand these cannot ignore the former. We cannot directly settle this matter in Aristotle's case, since too little is known about his life. But the self-sufficient substance and tremendous influence of his works over the centuries in spite this lack of biographical information suggest that the first attitude is more correct than the second. Aristotle's theoretical works can be and have been understood without knowing much about his life.

Can the same be said of the hero of this book, Ludwig Wittgenstein? I would suggest yes, but with an important qualification. He was one of the founders of analytic philosophy, and his main areas of research were theoretical and abstract: the foundations of mathematics and logic, philosophy of language and mind, and the nature of philosophy itself. True, Wittgenstein has come to be associated with postmodernism, art, poetry, mysticism, ethics, even politics. But in fact, what he wrote on these topics, from a philosophical point of view, amounts to a tiny fragment of a huge oeuvre. The true coordinates of the *Tractatus Logico-Philosophicus*, Wittgenstein's first book, to mention one example, are not Joyce, Schönberg or Picasso (as Terry Eagleton has claimed), but really Gottlob Frege and Bertrand Russell, two of the greatest logicians and philosophers of modern times. There is thus an imbalance between Wittgenstein's present-day public persona and the character of his actual work, which this book attempts to correct.

The qualification comes from the fact that Wittgenstein lived in the modern age, the age of intellectuals, of charismatic writers, thinkers and artists whose lives capture the collective imagination, since they incorporate some of the deepest tensions of modernity, and maybe even suggest some solutions to them. Wittgenstein is of course such a charismatic intellectual figure. His lifelong concern with religious faith, his ethical struggles and failures, his upper-class background and his later rejection of it in favour of an almost monkish life, his quest for love and torment with sex, his talent for engineering and disgust for scientism, his criticism of the modern way of life, his ambiguous relation to psychoanalysis or communism, his ultra-modernist taste in architecture and his otherwise conservative artistic preferences – at least some of these aspects of his personality bring him close to us. Aristotle's life, even if we knew its details, would simply not appeal to us in the same way. Wittgenstein's life, by contrast, is of great concern, indeed would be so even if his manuscripts on language, mind, logic and mathematics had been lost. This probably explains why Wittgenstein the intellectual can appeal to wide audiences, even though Wittgenstein the philosopher is little known outside academia. Wittgenstein was born, worked, loved, searched for God, suffered and died.

This book tries to find a balance between Wittgenstein the philosopher and Wittgenstein the intellectual, although the greater emphasis lies on the latter. It is also the intellectual who will, occasionally, be discussed from a more critical perspective. Two chapters are dedicated to his major books, the *Tractatus* and the *Philosophical Investigations*, but a critical discussion of his philosophy cannot be undertaken here. The book owes much to the seminal biographies by Brian McGuinness and Ray Monk, who have undertaken a great and ingenious effort to display the unity between Wittgenstein's personality and philosophy. If my approach differs slightly in stressing some discontinuities as well, it has only been possible through an aspect-shift that takes their biographies as points of departure.

Only from the consciousness of the uniqueness of my life *arises religion – science – and art.*
Ludwig Wittgenstein, *Notebooks*, 1 August 1916

You want to be perfect? – Of course I want to be perfect!
Ludwig Wittgenstein to Fania Pascal

1

Family and Early Years, 1889–1911

Ludwig Wittgenstein (1889–1951) was born and grew up in Vienna. It is not surprising that one of the most important philosophers in the modern age originated from this fabled metropolis. In the last decades before the First World War, Vienna was at the height of its imperial splendour, the capital of a vast and heterogeneous empire. It was one of the main cultural centres of the world, a melting pot of pathbreaking artistic and intellectual currents, a place where the stiffest conservatism clashed with the most radical modernism, where the demise of the old world and the hope for a new beginning were sensed most vividly, a place rife with contradictions, obsessions and genius. Sigmund Freud developed psychoanalysis in Vienna, Arnold Schönberg atonal music, Adolf Loos functionalist architecture, Gustav Klimt Secessionism, Arthur Schnitzler his taboo-breaking theatre and Karl Kraus his apocalyptic satire, to name but a few.[1] It was also a place of political 'innovation', if we are to count not only Theodor Herzl's Zionism and Victor Adler's and Otto Bauer's versions of socialism, but also the populist exploitation of anti-Semitism by the mayor Karl Lueger and the formation of Adolf Hitler's ideology during his Viennese apprenticeship years. Some of the most remarkable but also darker aspects of Ludwig Wittgenstein's personality can be traced back to this *fin-de-siècle* world, its refined sense of culture, its strict sense of duty, its cult of genius and tragedy, its awareness of a world in disintegration, and maybe to its sexual repression and anti-Semitism.

The Wittgenstein family's ancestors were Jewish. Ludwig's paternal great-grandfather, Moses Maier, lived in county Wittgenstein in Germany, now part of North Rhine–Westphalia, and was a land agent to the princely family Sayn-Wittgenstein. The family did not have aristocratic roots, although this was rumoured at times. Rather, Moses Maier took over the name 'Wittgenstein' following Napoleon's decree that all Jews must adopt a surname. What is certain is that Moses's son and Ludwig's grandfather, Hermann Christian Wittgenstein (1802–1878), converted to Protestantism, cut off his ties with the local Jewish community and moved to Leipzig, where he became a successful wool merchant. He was described as stiff and irascible, but also as determined and very religious, viewing life as a calling to self-accomplishment. In 1838 he married Fanny Figdor (1814–1890), the daughter of a rich, highly cultivated Viennese family, who, like him, renounced her Jewish faith and converted. The break with Judaism seems to have been so complete that Hermann Christian forbade his children to marry Jews. Indeed, he seems even to have been known as an anti-Semite, a state of mind that was not rare among converted Jews at the time. When they moved from Leipzig to Vienna in the 1850s the Wittgensteins did not participate in the Jewish community, but gave their children a thorough Germanic education. Through Fanny's family the Wittgensteins maintained close connections to the Viennese cultural and artistic elite. They were known as art collectors and as patrons of music. The famous violinist Joseph Joachim was adopted by Fanny and Hermann at a young age and sent to Leipzig to study with Felix Mendelssohn. Johannes Brahms was among numerous famous friends, giving piano lessons to the Wittgenstein daughters. The playwrights Franz Grillparzer and Christian Friedrich Hebbel were two other such illustrious friends. This privileged education and cultural exposure contrasted with the otherwise frugal regime that the children were deliberately brought up in.

The Wittgenstein family house, the 'Palais Wittgenstein' in Vienna.

Out of the ten children of the couple, Karl (1847–1913), Ludwig's father, was the most remarkable. He was rebellious, highly intelligent, good-looking, self-confident, impatient (especially with things he considered a waste of time, such as philosophy), at times frightening. In her unpublished memoirs his daughter Margarete writes that she had almost only sombre memories about her childhood. 'I did not deem the often irradiating gaiety of my father funny, but frightening.'[2] Karl was also practically minded and determined to make his own way – if necessary, against his father's or anybody else's wishes. As a teenager he ran away from home twice, the second time just after he had been expelled from school for denying the immortality of the soul in an essay. He ended up in

New York, where he worked as a waiter, violinist and teacher of music, mathematics and other subjects, finally returning home after two years with some money earned by himself and an invaluable experience of the New World. In later years he repeatedly praised the free market system in newspaper articles, while the Socialist press criticized his aggressive business methods, denouncing him as an 'American'. He studied engineering and worked first as a draughtsman in the railways, then in the construction of ships and turbines. At 27 he was the managing director of a Viennese company and from then it took him only two decades to become a steel magnate, heading several companies and turning into one of the wealthiest industrialists in Europe, much like Andrew Carnegie in America, whom he in fact befriended. Indeed, the family had the byname the 'Carnegies' of Central Europe before the war. At the age of 52 Karl Wittgenstein suddenly retired from business and transferred most of his fortune into US equities, which would make his family even richer with the onset of the economic depression following the First World War, and devoted his time to his family, to art and to writing sharp-witted political and economic articles for various periodicals. Although he refused the offer of being ennobled by adding a 'von' to his name (as this would have betrayed the parvenu), he lived in Vienna with his family in an aristocratic mansion, known as 'Palais Wittgenstein', built in the nineteenth century by a Hungarian count, and also possessed a house in Neuwaldegg on the outskirts of the capital, where Ludwig was born. In the summer the family would retreat to the Hochreit, Karl's country estate and hunting lodge in the mountains. As a patron of the arts he showed sensitivity for innovative developments, funding, for instance, the famous Sezession building, befriending the first president of the Vienna Secession group, Gustav Klimt, and generally surrounding himself and his family with the *crème de la crème* of the Viennese elite. 'The minister of fine art', as Klimt called Karl, acquired a large collection of art pieces,

Wittgenstein's parents. His father was a leading industrialist, his mother an accomplished pianist.

by Klimt himself, by Rodin, Max Klinger and others. Besides the grand old man Brahms, musicians such as Bruno Walter, Clara Schumann, Gustav Mahler, Josef Labor and Pablo Casals were also close to the family.

Karl had eight children with his wife Leopoldine Kalmus (1850–1926), whose parents both came from prominent Catholic families. Her father, however, had Jewish ancestors and so three of Ludwig's grandparents had Jewish ancestry. In conformity with their mother's denomination, Ludwig and his siblings were baptized into the Catholic faith, but there seems to have been little churchgoing in the family. Although fully devoted, indeed subservient to her husband, Leopoldine's relations with her children were not the warmest and they were, typically for a family of this social status, surrounded by nursemaids and private teachers most of the time. But there was one exception to this, and that was music. Leopoldine was an extremely gifted pianist and devoted much time to the musical education of her children. She was also a merciless critic. Often after a concert of the Vienna Philharmonic a large circle of music experts would gather in the Palais Wittgenstein and analyse the performance, with Leopoldine dominating such occasions, perhaps not unlike Ludwig many years later in Cambridge's philosophy circles. She was considered such a good pianist that some liked her playing better than that of her son Paul, the celebrated concert pianist. Most of her children were musically very talented and active, but her two sons Hans and Paul were exceptional. Hans was a pianist of genius, who gave public performances even as a child.

> A story [Ludwig] told in later life concerned an occasion when he was woken at three in the morning by the sound of a piano. He went downstairs to find Hans performing one of his own compositions. Hans's concentration was manic. He was sweating, totally absorbed, and completely oblivious of Ludwig's presence. The image remained for Ludwig a paradigm for what it was like to be possessed of genius.[3]

But his father was unmoved by this talent and had decided that his son should follow a business career. The conflict between the duty felt towards his father and his own calling caused severe tensions in Hans. Eventually, he ran away from home and ended up in the United States. He vanished from a boat at the age of 26 in Chesapeake Bay, an event that was interpreted as suicide.

Of Karl's five sons, two more, Rudolf and Kurt, committed suicide and Ludwig too would contemplate suicide throughout his life. Such events suggest that, despite all its cultural sophistication, there was something tragic, ruptured and morbid about this family, a good illustration of the thesis *Tiefenpsychologie* that Freud developed in Vienna, not by coincidence. As Brian McGuinness once

Wittgenstein with his brother Paul and sisters.

put it, the family history 'contains many anecdotes that may have figured in the appendices to a treatise on psycho-analysis'.[4] Rudolf, whose greatest interests were literature and theatre, was psychologically unstable. He suffered from the thought that he was a homosexual (a 'perverted disposition', as he described it in his farewell letter) and when he seemed to be unable to cope with his life in Berlin he ended it. He walked into a pub, ordered drinks, asked the pianist to play the song 'I am lost' and poisoned himself on the spot. He too had come into conflict with his father's expectations. Although the same is not true of Kurt, who killed himself because his soldiers deserted him while he was serving as an officer in the army on the Italian front in 1918, all these suicides betray an almost unbearable sense of duty, be it towards themselves or towards the overpowering father figure – a sense of duty that would sooner or later crush them.

Since the daughters did not experience the same kind of pressure from their father, their lives followed a more balanced pattern. Hermine organized musical evenings, helped her father in acquiring

Gustav Klimt, *Margarete Stonborough-Wittgenstein*, 1905, oil on canvas. Margarete was one of Wittgenstein's sisters.

his extensive picture collection and writing his autobiography, and later managed a day-care centre for children. She wrote a book about the family (*Recollections*) that contains insightful portraits and numerous fascinating anecdotes. She never married, but was considered the most harmonious person in the family. Helene did marry. She had great musical talents, but did not use them professionally. She also had a sense of humour that Ludwig could relate to, since she liked to play nonsensical games with language, which led to many funny exchanges with her philosopher brother, who was later to say that one could write a good philosophical book consisting entirely of jokes. But his closest affinity was with his youngest sister, Margarete ('Gretl'), a beautiful woman with a strong personality, sharp, critical intellect, a predilection for artistic innovation and passion for new ideas such as psychoanalysis. She was to become a friend of Sigmund Freud, who psychoanalysed her and whom she helped to flee the Nazis. Margarete exercised a great intellectual and artistic influence on her brother Ludwig. As Hermine wrote about her:

> Already in her youth her room was the embodied rebellion against anything traditional and the opposite of a typical young woman's room, as mine was for a long time. God knows where she found all those interesting objects with which she decorated her room. She was brimming with ideas and, most important, she could achieve what she wanted and she knew what she wanted.[5]

She married a wealthy American in 1905, Jerome Stonborough, and Klimt was commissioned to draw her wedding portrait, a painting that is now one of his most famous.

As a result of the tragic deaths of Hans and Rudolf, the younger sons Paul and Ludwig were treated differently. Paul, two years older than Ludwig, received a classical education and was allowed to pursue a career as a concert pianist and piano teacher. This career was tragically blighted when he lost his right arm in the First World War. Nevertheless, having a strong will, like so many of his relatives, he did not give up and learned to play with his left hand alone. He even commissioned special works from composers such as Richard Strauss, Sergej Prokofiev, Benjamin Britten and especially Maurice Ravel, who wrote the famous *Concerto for the Left Hand* (1932) for Paul. Here is what Ludwig told Maurice Drury about Paul in 1935:

> [Wittgenstein] said that his brother had the most amazing knowledge of music. On one occasion some friends played a few bars of music from any one of a number of composers, from widely different periods, and his brother was able without a mistake to say who the composer was and from which work it was taken. On the other hand he did not like his brother's interpretation of music. Once when his brother was practising the piano and Wittgenstein was in another room of the house, the music suddenly stopped and his brother burst into the room saying: 'I can't play when you are in the house. I feel your scepticism seeping under the door.'[6]

The youngest of the eight children, Ludwig Wittgenstein was born on 26 April 1889 (within days of Charlie Chaplin and Adolf Hitler and in the same year as Martin Heidegger). He was a delicate and sensitive child who was in constant need of protection. After receiving private tuition up to the age of 14, he was sent in 1903 to a *Realschule* in Linz specializing in scientific and technical education, a school of a lesser standard than the one Paul was sent to and where most of whose pupils were drawn from the working class. This school has achieved some notoriety because it was also attended by Adolf Hitler in the years 1900–04. Wittgenstein and Hitler were therefore at the same school for one year. Although born in the same year, Hitler attended school two years below Wittgenstein. We have no evidence that they talked to each other, an unlikely event given that both were loners, but it is not impossible that they knew each other, or at least that one knew of the other. Hitler

The young Wittgenstein on a rocking-horse, 1891.

writes in *Mein Kampf* that there was a Jewish boy at his school who was not much to be trusted and of whom Hitler thought little. Much has been made of this passage by an interpreter who claims that Wittgenstein was the boy mentioned by Hitler and that we can see them together in a class photo.[7] Moreover, Hitler was supposedly even influenced in his anti-Semitism by the awkward behaviour of his schoolmate Wittgenstein. The first claim is simply false (the boy supposedly identified as Wittgenstein in the photo is not him) and the second unconvincing speculation. If aspects of Hitler's ideology have their roots at this school, then they are more likely to be found in what the history teacher Leopold Pötsch taught Hitler, namely that the traditional patriotism for the Austro-Hungarian empire was obsolete and that the emerging pan-Germanic nationalism should be embraced instead.[8] The foundations of Hitler's anti-Semitism were not laid in Linz, but much more likely in Vienna, a city in which Austro-German xenophobia and especially anti-Semitism was rife, particularly during the long service of the populist mayor Karl Lueger (1897–1910), much admired by Hitler.[9]

With his reclusive character and his elitist background Ludwig did not adapt well to the new environment. He was later to describe his three years at the school as a painful experience, which would have been beset with total loneliness and alienation had it not been for the son of his host family with whom he developed a close friendship. As Hermine was later told by one of Ludwig's former classmates, he had appeared to them 'as if blown from an alien world. He had a completely different life-style from theirs, addressing his school-fellows . . . with the formal pronoun "Sie"; which created a barrier.' He read different books and appeared more mature and serious than them. 'Above all he was uncommonly sensitive, and I can imagine that to him his school-fellows in turn seemed to stem from another world, from a terrible one!'[10] They paid him back by ridiculing him with jingles such as 'Wittgenstein wends his woeful windy way towards Vienna'.[11] His performance at school was mediocre. He did well only in English and Conduct, and in Religion, where he scored the highest mark. Ironically it was in these years that he lost the naïve religious faith of his childhood, especially through conversations with Margarete. Nevertheless, questions of religious faith were to concern him for the rest of his life, if only rarely from a philosophical point of view.

Part of the reason that Ludwig was sent to this school was that, unlike his older brothers, he did not rebel against his father, although he would have been in the best position to get away with it. Instead, he seems to have manifested a concern with how he appeared in the eyes of others and thus a tendency to please everybody. At least this is how he perceived himself much later in a written confession addressed to his family:

As far as my memory goes I was an affectionate child but at the same time of weak character. Very early in life I recognised the

Wittgenstein as a teenager.

greater strength of character of my brother Paul. When he had been slightly sick and was recovering and was asked whether he would like to get up now or would prefer to stay longer in bed, he would calmly say that he would rather stay lying down; whereas I in the same circumstances said what was untrue (that I wanted to get up) because I was afraid of the bad opinion of those around me.[12]

There may be some truth in this self-description. But we should bear in mind that it is written by a merciless prosecutor, an author who, like Augustine in his *Confessions*, excelled in self-accusations and agonized endlessly over his real and perceived sins. This

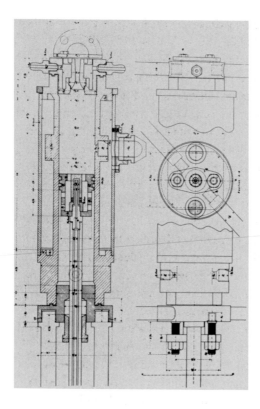

An engineering diagram drawn by the young Wittgenstein.

extreme concern with one's moral status can be seen as partly inherited from the family, if we remember the troubled souls of his brothers Hans and Rudolf, and the sense of duty present in the family. But only partly. Not every moral trait is inherited, and exemplary figures such as Augustine or Wittgenstein are cases in their own class who do not just embody typical moral problems, but also deepen human morality and offer new ways of understanding it.

What is certain, however, is that Ludwig's cultural formation was to a large extent determined by his upbringing. As part of the Austro-German education received by the whole family, the boy was taught the canon of classic German literature, that is, Goethe, Schiller, Lessing, Mörike, authors he would admire for the rest of his life. He was also very fond of Lichtenberg's aphorisms, which he would quote in his diaries, and of Schopenhauer and Gottfried Keller. His literary taste could be described as conservative. He became familiar with the works of nineteenth-century writers such as Johann Nestroy, Grillparzer and Nikolaus Lenau, and, also, largely through Margarete's influence, with Freud's progressive ideas and Karl Kraus's scathing and stylistically brilliant criticism of moral, intellectual and linguistic decadence. But he never warmed to the authors of his own generation. The most modern writers he admired were Tolstoy, Dostoevsky, Kierkegaard and Nietzsche. All he had to say about Kafka was that this was some-body who gave 'himself a great deal of trouble *not* writing about his trouble'.[13] He did read Thomas Mann, Rainer Maria Rilke and Georg Trakl, and he did acknowledge genius where he sensed it (for instance in Trakl), but none of these became favourites.

The same holds for his musical orientation. Although the period of his youth was a time of great innovation in music, especially in Vienna, where the Second Viennese School around Arnold Schoenberg, Alban Berg and Anton Webern developed twelve-tone music, Wittgenstein's taste remained more traditional. This was not because he had no understanding of music. Although he did not learn to play any instrument in his childhood, he was, like the rest of his family, musically very gifted and could whistle whole scores with great accuracy. As an adult he taught himself the clarinet. Wittgenstein simply detested contemporary music. Even a composer like Gustav Mahler was too modern and corrupted for him, and he would enter violent arguments with anybody who thought otherwise.[14] His heroes were Haydn, Mozart, Beethoven, Schubert, Brahms and Labor (the latter was patronized by Ludwig's father). An exception regarding Wittgenstein's anti-modernist tastes was architecture, about which more will be said later.

There is one further contemporary influence that needs to be mentioned in this context, and it is one of darker provenance: Otto Weininger's *Sex and Character* (1903). It is difficult for us today to understand the fascination this misogynistic, racist and reactionary book exercised, not only on young Wittgenstein but on a whole generation. Weininger (1880–1903) was a tormented homosexual and anti-Semitic young Jew who at the age of 23, only half a year after his book was published (and half a year before Rudolf Wittgenstein killed himself in a similarly theatrical manner), committed suicide in the house in which Beethoven had died in Vienna. This suicide made Weininger immediately famous, and his book became a bestseller, reaching thirteen reprints within four years. The book pretends to give a complete anthropology, a solution to all moral problems and an intransigent critique of modernity. Humans are bipolar beings, torn apart between the pursuit for higher ideals, such as truth and love, and mere animal instincts such as sexuality. Love and sex are thus mutually exclusive. The first corresponds to the Platonic form of 'Man', the second to that of 'Woman'. All humans are mixtures of these two forms and thus bisexual, but actual women embody 'Woman' to a much larger degree. Women are therefore akin to animals, entirely concerned with the 'main' aspects of sexuality, procreation and motherhood. Men are concerned with much more spiritual things, for example, politics, philosophy, art. Only they possess rationality, morality and free will, whereas women are immoral and herd animals. Jews are entirely female ('the most manly Jew is more feminine than the least manly Aryan')[15] and thus entirely depraved.

As Ray Monk explains, it could not be Weininger's anti-Semitism or 'theory' of women that attracted Wittgenstein.[16] Later in life he actually said about this 'theory': 'How wrong [Weininger] was, my God he was wrong.'[17] It was rather Weininger's views on men and modernity, and the more general ethical questions Weininger raised (as Wittgenstein tried to explain later to his puzzled

The Austrian writer Otto Weininger, an influence on Wittgenstein.

Cambridge friends). The modern age is an age of depravity and decay, of the masses, of materialism, science, communism and capitalism. It is an age of the disappearance of the spirit, of morality, art and genius. The only way to reverse this is open to men, to a *few* men, who rise above mediocrity, aspire to realize the divine in themselves and acquire genius. This could only be achieved through real love:

> If we now turn to the gifted, we shall see that in their case love frequently begins with self-mortification, humiliation, and

Wittgenstein and his friend Eccles experimenting with a kite on the moors near Glossop, Derbyshire, in 1908.

restraint. A moral change sets in, a process of purification seems to emanate from the object loved.[18]

We find aspects of Weininger's *Kulturkritik* in other writers Wittgenstein read, such as Nietzsche and Kraus. But none offered so radical a choice as Weininger, namely that between genius and death. Weininger's own suicide can be seen as the logical consequence of this, once he realized that he could not, by his own nature, become a genius. This insistence on the duties to oneself, on radical honesty and the obsession with suicide as the ultimate conclusion in the face of failure is something we find Wittgenstein preoccupied with from 1903 to 1912 – the time he entered school in Linz to his realization in Cambridge that he was capable of something original after all, namely original work in philosophy.

After he finished school in the summer of 1906 he went to Berlin to study mechanical engineering, a course to the liking of his father and one from which he graduated successfully in 1908. In Berlin he went numerous times to the opera, 30 times alone to hear Wagner's *Die Meistersinger*, if we are to believe him. It was also the time in which he started writing a diary, 'thoughts about myself on slips of paper', as he wrote in retrospect.

It was an important step for me. Later it came partly from an impulse to imitate (I had read Keller's diaries) and partly from the need to preserve something of myself. So it was in large part vanity. But it was also a substitute for a person in whom I could confide.[19]

In Berlin Wittgenstein became interested in aeronautics and after graduation, in 1908, he went to the University of Manchester to study this nascent field. He continued his research there for another three years, experimenting for a while with self-made kites at a meteorological observation station near Glossop, where he met William Eccles, an engineer with whom he stayed friends for three decades. Back in Manchester he began to design a jet-reaction propeller, whose engine he patented in 1911 and for which he earned a research studentship from the university. Clearly, he was showing talent and innovation. But by then engineering proved to be a dead end, given that his interest in philosophy had become overwhelming.

2

Cambridge, Norway and Philosophy, 1911–14

It is hard to pinpoint exactly when Wittgenstein became interested in philosophy. His interest in the general ethical questions such as those posed by Weininger occurred early on. He also read Schopenhauer in his early years. Schopenhauer stressed that life was futile and full of suffering, which could be overcome by art and especially by music, and his idealism must have appealed to the cultivated and lonesome teenager. But we also know that towards the end of his school days Wittgenstein considered studying with Ludwig Boltzmann in Vienna. Boltzmann was a prominent physicist who had invented statistical mechanics, but who was also known for his lectures on the philosophy of physics, some of which were published in his *Popular Writings* in 1905 and which Wittgenstein read. He also read the introduction to Heinrich Hertz's famous *Principles of Mechanics* (1894). Both Boltzmann and Hertz operated within a broadly Kantian framework, according to which science is a model constructed by the human mind that does not refer to or describe reality, but rather is used to organize empirical data in one among several possible ways. As Hertz argued, when we encounter a problem about a particular theoretical term, such as 'force', we should not ask whether something corresponds to this term in reality, but reformulate our scientific theory without using the term. (This came later to be known as 'instrumentalism' in the philosophy of science.) Hertz wrote: 'the question as to the nature of force will not have been answered; but our minds, no longer vexed, will cease to ask illegitimate questions'.[1] Wittgenstein knew passages such as this by heart and they became relevant for his own philosophy.

In any case, such readings show that by the time he went to Berlin his interests covered questions of a more theoretical nature than those related to engineering. In Berlin or very soon afterwards they must have turned into a calling. As Hermine wrote in her memoirs:

> At this period or a little later he was suddenly gripped by philosophy . . . so violently and so much against his will that he suffered severely from the twofold and conflicting inner vocation and seemed to himself to be torn in two. One of the many transformations he was to go through in his life had come over him and shook him to the depths of his being.[2]

Although it may be more appropriate to speak of a gradual process that eventually precipitated than of a sudden conversion to philosophy, this crisis was certainly genuine and only reinforced by the fact that his interest in philosophy also conflicted with the father's hope that at least one of the sons should do something meaningful.

In Manchester, and partly through his studies in aeronautics, Wittgenstein became interested in higher mathematics, attending E. J. Littlewood's lectures on the theory of mathematical analysis, and eventually in the foundations of mathematics. The foundations of mathematics was a field that, after a long period of neglect, had begun to receive great attention in the nineteenth century, particularly through the works of George Boole, Georg Cantor, Richard Dedekind, Gottlob Frege, Giuseppe Peano, Karl Weierstrass and others, and was still very much at the fore in the early twentieth century. At stake was the justification of mathematics as a scientific discipline. In particular, Gottlob Frege's (1848–1925) contribution to this debate, although neglected in his lifetime, turned out in

Part of a page from the German edition of Frege's *Basic Laws of Arithmetic*.

retrospect as the most pivotal, since his own answer to the foundational question led to the greatest revolution in logic since Aristotle. Frege's own theory of mathematics, so-called logicism, involved the idea that all truths of arithmetic are deducible from a few purely logical truths, which themselves are self-evident, indubitable and independent of the human mind. Logicism also involved the claim that numbers are genuine objects, although not physical or mental, but abstract ones, situated in a 'Third Realm'. Consequently, statements about numbers, for example, '1 + 2 = 3', are not statements about physical or mental objects such as a collection of apples on a table or of mental ideas in our mind or brain, but statements about certain abstract objects. In any case, in order to prove that arithmetic is deducible from logical laws alone, Frege devised an ideal language and a formal logical calculus much more powerful than the Aristotelian syllogistic available hitherto. He presented this logic in his *Concept Script* (1879), argued for his logicism in the *Foundations of Arithmetic* (1884) and finally came to develop it fully in his two-volume masterwork *Basic Laws of Arithmetic* (vol. I, 1893, vol. II, 1903). Both the propositional logic and the predicate logic

The philosopher and mathematician Gottlob Frege, a major influence on Wittgenstein.

taught at universities today go back to Frege's innovations. His reflections on language, which he published in several articles, are equally important and are considered classics in philosophy of language. Frege thought that our natural language, 'the language of the marketplace', as he called it, is vague, imprecise and misleading, and therefore not apt to articulate the logicist programme. Only the ideal language he developed to support his logical calculus could do that. Wittgenstein was to be deeply influenced by and take issue with many of Frege's claims.

   A programme similar to Frege's was pursued in England by Bertrand Russell (1872–1970), in *The Principles of Mathematics*

(1903) and later in *Principia Mathematica* (1910–13), co-authored with Alfred North Whitehead. In his famous article 'On Denoting' (1905) Russell argued that natural language is misleading and that its structure can be understood only by means of logical analysis. Thus he claimed that a sentence like 'The present king of France is bald' only appears to be an ordinary subject-predicate sentence, whereas in reality it is a much more complicated sentence. Russell thought that we can apply logic to ordinary sentences to unveil their real structure, in this way solving any problems that might arise from troublesome terms. The troublesome term here is 'The present king of France', which according to Russell must be viewed as meaningless, if it is taken as the grammatical subject, since there is no present king of France. And if a component of a sentence is meaningless, then the sentence itself must be meaningless. Thus it would seem that we must conclude from the meaninglessness of 'The present king of France' to the meaninglessness of 'The present king of France is bald'! But of course, the sentence 'The present king of France is bald' is *not* meaningless. We all understand it. Russell solved this problem by claiming that the sentence actually means 'There is one and only one king of France and he is bald' and that this is its actual, if more complicated form (which in the notation of mathematical logic looks even more complicated). Here the trouble-some term 'the present king of France' does not even occur and thus the problem this term posed does not arise anymore. This ingen-ious argument has some similarity to the way Hertz treated the term 'force', as just seen. With Russell's article the paradigm of philosophical analysis, which was to dominate much of twentieth-century Anglophone philosophy, was born. In his early period Wittgenstein accepted this paradigm, that is, that we can understand the real structure of our language only through logical analysis, and he came to reject it only much later (see chapter Eight).

Wittgenstein came across the works of Frege and Russell in Manchester for the first time and started very soon to come up

Bertrand Russell in 1918.

with solutions to various related questions. Russell had shown that Frege's system, as developed in his *Basic Laws of Arithmetic*, contained a disastrous flaw, since it was possible to derive a straightforward paradox from Frege's basic assumptions. For one could derive the existence of a set of all those sets that do not contain themselves as a member. What are we to say about this set then? Does it contain itself or not? If it contains itself, then it does not meet the initial requirement and thus it is not part of itself, that is, it does not contain itself. If, however, it does not contain itself, then it meets the initial requirement and thus it does contain itself. And so on. This set theoretic paradox plunged Frege into despair and he tried, unsuccessfully, to mend his system.[3] Russell's own solution to this problem involved the presupposition that there are infinitely many objects in the world (this is the so-called axiom of infinity), but Wittgenstein found this presupposition dubious as soon as he started thinking about this problem. As he was to say later, 'Logic

an illustration: "The author of Waverley was a poet." This implies (1) that
Waverley was written, (2) that it was written by one man, and not in collaboration, (3) that the one man who wrote it was a poet. If any one of these fails,
the proposition is false. Thus " the author of ' Slawkenburgius on Noses ' was
a poet " is false, because no such book was ever written; " the author of ' The
Maid's Tragedy ' was a poet " is false, because this play was written by
Beaumont and Fletcher jointly. These two possibilities of falsehood do not
arise if we say "Scott was a poet." Thus our interpretation of the uses of
$(\imath x)(\phi x)$ must be such as to allow for them. Now taking ϕx to replace
" x wrote Waverley," it is plain that any statement apparently about $(\imath x)(\phi x)$
requires (1) $(\exists x).(\phi x)$ and (2) $\phi x.\phi y.\supset_{x,y}.x=y$; here (1) states that *at
least* one object satisfies ϕx, while (2) states that *at most* one object satisfies
ϕx. The two together are equivalent to

$$(\exists c):\phi x.\equiv_x.x=c,$$

which we defined as $E!(\imath x)(\phi x).$

Part of a page from Whitehead's and Russell's *Principia Mathematica*.

must take care of itself '. It is an *a priori* discipline and it cannot
rely on any assumptions about the world, even about the number
of objects. Indeed, logic does not make a claim about anything.
It does not have a subject matter – a contention standing in stark
contrast to the beliefs of Frege ansd Russell that logic describes
the relations between 'logical objects' in a Platonistic 'Third Realm'
(Frege) or the most general features of the universe (Russell). The
truths of logic are tautologies, for example, 'Either it is raining or
it is not raining', and they are always true, but vacuously so. For to
know that it is either raining or it is not raining is not to know
anything about the world. These ideas, which came very early to
Wittgenstein, were later incorporated into the *Tractatus* and they
belong to the most significant aspects of his early philosophy.

Wittgenstein did not accept Russell's solution of the set theoretic
paradox. In April 1909, at the age of 20, he wrote to the mathematician Philip Jourdain, Russell's friend, proposing his own solution
to the paradox.[4] Jourdain, after consulting Russell, rejected this
solution, but Wittgenstein did not give up. He wrote to Frege and
visited him in Jena in 1911. It was an eye-opening experience.

I was shown into Frege's study. Frege was a small, neat man with a pointed beard who bounced around the room as he talked. He absolutely wiped the floor with me, and I felt very depressed; but at the end he said 'You must come again', so I cheered up. I had several discussions with him after that. Frege would never talk about anything but logic and mathematics, if I started on some other subject, he would say something polite and then plunge back into logic and mathematics. He once showed me an obituary on a colleague, who, it was said, never used a word without knowing what it meant; he expressed astonishment that a man should be praised for this!'[5]

Wittgenstein wanted to study with Frege, but Frege suggested that it would be better for the young man to go to Cambridge and work with Russell. Wittgenstein followed his advice. Although he was still a student in Manchester, he travelled to Cambridge in October 1911, went unannounced to the rooms of the famous philosopher and introduced himself. He started attending Russell's lectures, sometimes dominating them, after which he would follow Russell to his rooms and involve the latter in intense philosophical discussions till late at night. Initially, Russell seems to have been slightly irritated by his new student, as we can gather from his daily letters to his lover Lady Ottoline Morrell. Just one day after the initial meeting Russell wrote: 'My German friend threatens to be an infliction.' A few days later: 'My German, who seems to be rather good, was very argumentative.' Then again: 'My German engineer, I think, is a fool. He thinks nothing empirical is knowable – I asked him to admit that there was no rhinoceros in the room, but he wouldn't.' It may be easy to make fun of this exchange, as Russell seems to have done, but it does show that Wittgenstein came with his own philosophical views to Cambridge and was eager to defend them.[6]

At the end of Michaelmas term Wittgenstein wanted to know whether it made sense for him to continue philosophy and thus resolve the vocational crisis he had been in since he left school. He asked Russell for advice and Russell told him to give him some written work first. The essay Wittgenstein produced over the vacation much impressed Russell. As he wrote to Lady Ottoline, he thought it was 'very good, much better than my English pupils do. I shall certainly encourage him. Perhaps he will do great things.' He advised him to continue with philosophy, an encouragement that Wittgenstein perceived as his salvation, ending the uncertainty about his direction in life. On 1 February 1912 he was admitted as an undergraduate at Trinity College, with Russell as his supervisor. But this was no ordinary student. At the end of the term Russell realized that he had taught his pupil everything he himself knew and that Wittgenstein was '*the* young man one hopes for', who could solve the great philosophical problems Russell himself felt too exhausted to tackle after completing his masterwork *Principia Mathematica*.

> W. is very excitable: he has more passion about philosophy than I have; his avalanches make mine seem mere snowballs. He has the pure intellectual passion in the highest degree; it makes me love him. His disposition is that of an artist, intuitive and moody. He says every morning he begins his work with hope, and every evening he ends in despair.[7]

When Hermine Wittgenstein visited her brother in Cambridge at the end of Trinity term Russell told her that 'We expect the next big step in philosophy to be taken by your brother', which came as something of a shock to her, since her brother had not been regarded as anything out of the ordinary in their family hitherto. She also noticed how much happier Ludwig seemed to be in Cambridge. Even decades later, when Russell had come to be critical of Wittgenstein's later philosophy, he would write in his *Autobiography* that Wittgenstein was 'perhaps the most perfect example I have ever known of genius as traditionally conceived, passionate, profound, intense, and dominating'.[8] Russell and Wittgenstein were soon discussing philosophy as equals. As mentioned, Wittgenstein's initial interest had been in the philosophy of mathematics and the solution to Russell's Paradox. But in Cambridge he began to think about more questions, namely the nature of logic itself, its subject matter, the status of logical truths, the relation between logic and fundamental language. These questions were to preoccupy him for several years and he presented his answers in the *Tractatus*, completed in 1918.

Like Vienna, Cambridge before the First World War was a place of many renowned academics and intellectuals, and one could have expected Wittgenstein to fit well in this context. Given his depressive nature, this was only partly the case. But it was certainly helpful for Wittgenstein to be able to exchange with other high-calibre minds. Apart from Russell he became acquainted with leading figures such as the mathematician G. H. Hardy, the logician W. E. Johnson, and the philosophers Whitehead, J. E. McTaggart, George Edward Moore, and the great economist John Maynard Keynes. Whitehead and McTaggart did not have a favourable impression of the young philosopher. Johnson was initially appointed as Wittgenstein's personal tutor, but this arrangement was terminated after a few weeks, since Johnson was estranged by the student's patronizing behaviour. Nevertheless, they stayed on friendly terms. Over time, Wittgenstein also became friends with Moore and Keynes. Moore (1873–1958) had already published his most important contributions to the nascent current of analytic philosophy, in particular his book *Principia Ethica* (1903). Wittgenstein did not think too highly of Moore as a philosopher, but he admired Moore's sincerity and truthfulness. Keynes (1883–1946), who at the time was working on the theory of probability and was influenced by Russell and Moore, was fascinated by Wittgenstein as soon as they met. He was certainly Wittgenstein's intellectual match, quick,

sharp, original and open to new ideas, and in his first years in
Cambridge Wittgenstein spent countless hours in discussions with
him. Keynes was also to become one of Wittgenstein's protectors
on a more practical level, helping him when he became a prisoner
of war in 1918, bringing him back to Cambridge in 1929 and finally
lobbying for his professorship in 1939.

It was partly due to Keynes's support that Wittgenstein was
made a member of the Apostles in November 1912. This was a
select debating society founded in the nineteenth century, which
was presently led by Keynes and the writer Lytton Strachey, and
somebody like Wittgenstein was just the kind of member they were
after. Around the turn of the century some of the most famous
British intellectuals and writers were its members, including the
Bloomsbury generation. The Apostles adopted Wittgenstein as an
'embryo', which was the first step towards full membership. Russell
was opposed to this adoption, arguing that the 'embryo' would not
like their intellectual and homoerotic self-affectation. And, indeed,
Wittgenstein was disgusted by the society and left it after only one
term. The one thing the Apostles were not, he said, was apostolic.
A sample of the pretentious tone among the Apostles is given by
the following passage from a letter by Strachey to Keynes, dated
17 May 1912:

> Oliver and Herr Sinckel-Winckel [Wittgenstein] hard at it on
> universals and particulars. The latter oh! so bright – but quelle
> souffrance! Oh God! God! 'If A loves B' – 'There may be a com-
> mon quality' – 'Not analysable that way at all, but the complexes
> have certain qualities.' How shall I manage to slink off to bed?[9]

More committed was Wittgenstein's participation in the meetings
of the Moral Science Club, the university's philosophy society.
With Moore's help he even changed the rules of the society to
improve the quality of the discussions, establishing a chairman to

A group photograph of the Cambridge University Moral Science Club, *c.* 1913.

keep the debating on target and stipulating that no paper should
be longer than seven minutes. In December he gave his first philosophical talk, on the question 'What is Philosophy?', which lasted
just four minutes, beating the previous record by two minutes.
In this talk he argued that philosophy is the totality of all propositions that are taken as unprovable and basic in science.

Wittgenstein's closest personal friend was, however, not an
established don, but a young man he met through Russell in 1912,
David Pinsent, a brilliant undergraduate in mathematics (and
descendant of David Hume). Pinsent assisted Wittgenstein in certain experiments involving the role of rhythm in the appreciation of
music at the psychological laboratory, a topic Wittgenstein became
interested in upon meeting the experimental psychologist C. S.
Myers. These experiments showed that under certain conditions
subjects are prone to hear a rhythm in a sequence of beats that is
not really there. It appears that Wittgenstein gave a paper on this
topic at the British Psychological Association in Cambridge in 1912.
Whether he intended this work to have any philosophical significance is not certain. It may have been the parallel between music

Wittgenstein's friend David Pinsent, to whom the *Tractatus Logico-Philosophicus* was to be dedicated, seen here in Norway on a trip with Wittgenstein.

and language to which Wittgenstein was drawn, as McGuinness suggests.[10] But it may have also been mere curiosity for a phenomenon that had both a scientific and an aesthetic aspect and thus fitted with Wittgenstein's general interests. In any case, it was through these experiments and the love for music that he found an intimate friend in Pinsent. In character very different from Wittgenstein, enthusiastic, unaffected, not easily disturbed, Pinsent proved the ideal companion until his untimely death in 1918. Wittgenstein called him 'my first and only friend' and dedicated the *Tractatus* to him. They spent much time together, going to concerts, playing music, even going on trips to Iceland and Norway. Pinsent kept a diary covering his friendship with Wittgenstein, which contains much invaluable information about young Ludwig.

Wittgenstein soon confided in Pinsent as in no one else before, telling him about the loneliness and suicidal thoughts he had experienced since leaving his parents' home in 1903, thoughts from which he was relieved only in Cambridge. The two friends also had many conversations about philosophy. In May 1912 Pinsent wrote in his diary: 'he is reading philosophy . . . but has only just started systematic reading: and he expresses the most naïve surprise that all the philosophers he once worshipped in ignorance are after all stupid and dishonest and make disgusting mistakes!'[11] A year later, in August 1913, Pinsent notes:

> he explained to me his latest discoveries in logic. They are truly amazing and have solved all the problems on which he has been working unsatisfactorily for the last year. . . . Of course he has upset a lot of Russell's work – but Russell would be the last to resent that, and really the greatness of his work suffers little thereby – as it is obvious that Wittgenstein is one of Russell's disciples and owes enormously to him. But Wittgenstein's work is really amazing – and I really believe that the mucky morass of Philosophy is at last crystallizing about a rigid theory of Logic – the only portion of Philosophy about which there is a possibility of man knowing anything . . . Really Logic is all Philosophy. All else that is loosely so termed is either metaphysics – which is hopeless, there being no data – or Natural Science e.g. Psychology.[12]

Pinsent's diaries also give insight into some of the more eccentric sides of Wittgenstein's personality. After he was offered accommodation at Trinity College, Wittgenstein went on a shopping tour for furniture with Pinsent. 'I went out and helped him interview a lot of furniture at various shops . . . It was rather amusing: he is terribly fastidious and we led the shopman a frightful dance, Vittgenstein [sic] ejaculating "No – Beastly!" to 90% of what he shewed us!'[13] Around the same time Wittgenstein told Russell that 'he dislikes all ornamentation that is not part of the construction, and can never find anything simple enough'.[14] This was of course the taste of Kraus and Loos, for whom ornament was the expression of inauthenticity and decadence. Eventually Wittgenstein decided to have the furniture specially made for him. In an earlier episode Wittgenstein and Eccles, his friend from Manchester, were planning to catch a train from Manchester to Liverpool. However, having missed the train, Wittgenstein suggested hiring an entire train to bring them to their destination. The plan was eventually dropped, but he still opted for a costly solution, namely hiring a taxi. These incidents prove that in his earlier years Wittgenstein was not quite the hermit he was to become after the First World War. When he asked Pinsent to accompany him on a trip to Iceland in September 1912, Pinsent's reply was that he was unsure whether he could afford the trip. But Wittgenstein told him not to worry, because, while he himself had no money either, his father 'had plenty of it'. He then handed over a considerable amount of cash to Pinsent. When the journey started, Wittgenstein was

> very fussy about taking enough clothing: he himself has three bags of luggage, and is much perturbed by my single box. He made me buy a second rug in Cambridge and several other odds and ends in Edinborough [sic] this morning – especially as it is not my money I am thus spending.[15]

During the Iceland trip Wittgenstein proved to be an interesting if very intense and occasionally difficult travel companion. Together they explored the countryside on ponies during the day and in the evening Wittgenstein taught Pinsent logic. The friends had several arguments, some on topics of general interest, for instance over women's suffrage (Wittgenstein was against it) and public schools (he accused them of cruelty and indifference to suffering), but also some personal ones, which were always started by Wittgenstein. Unlike Pinsent, he was irascible and could perceive innocent acts as entirely offensive. Thus when Pinsent entered a conversation with another traveller on the train and went to have a smoke with him in another carriage, Wittgenstein became furious, throwing what can only be described as a fit of jealousy and telling Pinsent that if he pleased he could travel the whole day with the other man. Thanks to Pinsent's frankness and friendliness they soon made up again, but there were other occurrences of what Pinsent called 'sulky fits' during the trip. It has been suggested that the two friends were really lovers, but there is no evidence for this. It seems more accurate to say that for Wittgenstein, his relationship with Pinsent had a very different significance than it had for the latter. As McGuinness has suggested, for Pinsent the friendship was following a conventional pattern; it was the kind of friendship a former public schoolboy like him would have with a person he had known only for a few months.[16] There may have been suppressed erotic undertones on Wittgenstein's side – a leitmotif in Wittgenstein's relations with other young men, in which the homoerotic charge was often only experienced by Wittgenstein, and rarely expressed. Of far greater, indeed tremendous, importance to him was closeness on both a spiritual and personal level.

Wittgenstein was a very intense human being, 'he had the idea of perfection in every area, in the serious matters of everyday life, in his work, or in the choice of a handkerchief for a present'.[17] Once, when he was pacing 'up and down in my [Russell's] room like a wild beast for three hours in agitated silence', Russell asked him whether he was thinking about logic or his sins, to which Wittgenstein replied 'Both.' He could only tolerate total sincerity and did not accept compromises about anything, be it personal, philosophical or aesthetic matters. If such disagreements arose, he would not only be entirely frank with the other person to the point of disregarding their feelings, but even try to change their life. It is reported that when, during his first year in Cambridge, he found out that a certain undergraduate was a monk, Wittgenstein, disapproving of the dishonesty he saw in any organized form of religion, fiercely attacked the man in the presence of others, telling him that he should read some good book on exact science to see what honest thought really is. Or again, after attending Moore's lectures in October 1912, Wittgenstein, officially only an undergraduate, sharply criticized the much more senior philosopher. 'He told me these lectures were very bad – that what I ought to do was to say what *I* thought, not to discuss what other people thought; and he came no more to my lectures.'[18]

This frankness, paired with his quick-tempered and overbearing nature, was not tolerated by everybody. In Wittgenstein's second year in Cambridge personal frictions emerged between him and Russell. One immediate reason was Wittgenstein's disapproval of Russell's essay 'The Essence of Religion' (1912), in which he attempted to formulate a new mysticism based on the 'infinite part of our life'. Wittgenstein fiercely attacked Russell for betraying the spirit of exactness and speaking in public in a fuzzy way about very intimate issues. 'Wittgenstein's criticism disturbed me profoundly. He was so unhappy, so gentle, so wounded in his wish to think well of me.'[19] Soon after they went to watch a boat race. Wittgenstein's reaction, according to Russell, was to say that '*all* was of the devil':

> he suddenly stood still and explained that the way we had spent the afternoon was so vile that we ought not to live, or at least he ought not, that nothing is tolerable except producing great works or enjoying those of others, that he has accomplished nothing and never will, etc. – all this with a force that knocks one down. He makes me feel like a bleating lambkin.[20]

But eventually these scenes became too much even for Russell. On one occasion he told his pupil to stop thinking so much about himself, and on another he suggested that Wittgenstein read some French prose in order to escape the 'danger of becoming narrow and uncivilised' by focusing only on logic. Wittgenstein took such advice badly. Some months later, in June 1913, Wittgenstein came to Russell to analyse their relationship, pointing out what he thought was going wrong between them. After unsuccessfully trying to calm down his pupil Russell finally said sharply: 'All you want is a little self-control.' Upon this Wittgenstein left the room 'in an air of high tragedy', failed to show up at a concert they planned to attend together, and Russell had to look for him, fearing he might commit suicide.

What also strained the relationship was the fact that the younger philosopher became more and more critical of Russell's ideas and began to develop an increasingly original account of logic. So dominating and dismissive was Wittgenstein in their conversations that Russell stopped talking about his work at one point. When he did show Wittgenstein a manuscript on the theory of knowledge he was working on, the reaction was merciless:

> He said it was all wrong, not realizing the difficulties – that he had tried my view and knew it wouldn't work. I couldn't understand his objection . . . but I feel in my bones that he must be right, and that he has seen something I have missed. . . . I feel it is probably all wrong, and that Wittgenstein will think me a dishonest scoundrel for going on with it.[21]

In retrospect Russell judged this criticism as an event of 'first-rate importance' in his life, since it made him realize he could not do any fundamental work in philosophy again. 'My impulse was shattered, like a wave dashed to pieces against a breakwater. I became filled with utter despair.'[22] Russell stopped work on his manuscript and it was published only posthumously.

Wittgenstein's second year in Cambridge was marked by progress in his own philosophical activity. The Christmas break of

1912–13, which he spent in the family retreat on the Hochreit and thus far removed from any academic environment, proved to be fruitful, and upon his return he reported his progress to Russell. In March 1913 Wittgenstein's first publication came out, a short review of a logic textbook by P. Coffey written for the *Cambridge Review*. The sharply critical review, the only one of its kind he ever wrote, smacked of overconfidence:

> In no branch of learning can an author disregard the results of honest research with so much impunity as he can in Philosophy and Logic. To this circumstance we owe the publication of such a book as Mr Coffey's 'Science of Logic': and only as a typical example of the work of many logicians of to-day does this book deserve consideration. . . . The author has not taken the slightest notice of the great work of the modern mathematical logicians – work which has brought about an advance in Logic comparable only to that which made Astronomy out of Astrology, and Chemistry out of Alchemy. . . . The worst of such books as this is that they prejudice sensible people against the study of Logic.[23]

It is noteworthy that in this review Wittgenstein presented himself as belonging to the camp of the modern logicians, that is, Russell and Frege, although at the same time he was engaged in a thorough revision of their accounts of logic. Despite his growing criticism of these thinkers, his reverence for them was unbroken. This can also be seen from the fact that in the same year he translated parts of Frege's *Basic Laws of Arithmetic* in collaboration with Philip Jourdain (the translation was published in *The Monist* under Jourdain's name).

The summer vacation, half of which was spent on the Hochreit again, while the other half with Pinsent in Norway, was very productive. The choice of Norway, a place he would visit many times henceforth, is telling.[24] Initially, the two friends had planned to go to Spain, but the philosophical progress he had achieved on the Hochreit led Wittgenstein to a change of mind. He now preferred a quiet holiday allowing for opportunity to work to a voyage full of distractions, during which he might have been surrounded 'by crowds of American tourists, which he can't stand' (as Pinsent reports). The trip was more enjoyable than the previous one to Iceland. Wittgenstein was now a more amicable companion, although some 'sulky fits' still occurred. They travelled comfortably, mostly in first class, and eventually found a quiet village, Øystese, in a fjord near Bergen, where they spent three weeks. They played dominoes, went on walking tours, but also spent a considerable amount of time working. Wittgenstein was trying to solve certain difficult problems about the foundations of logic and this visibly required all his concentration. As Pinsent describes it, Wittgenstein would mutter 'to himself in a mixture of German and English' and 'stride up and down the room all the while'.[25]

The progress Wittgenstein made during this vacation gave him some confidence that he was doing something worthwhile. He felt that his ideas were original and significant enough to be important to *others*. But this progress also gave him reason to agonize; for his valuable ideas could be lost. In his letters to Russell he wrote:

I very often now have the indescribable feeling as though my work was all sure to be lost entirely in some way or other. But I still hope this won't come true. Whatever happens don't forget me!' (5 September 1913)

I have had all sorts of ideas which seem to me very fundamental. Now the feeling that I shall have to die before able to publish them is growing stronger in me every day and my greatest wish would therefore be to communicate *everything* that I have done so far to you *as soon as possible*. (20 September 1913)[26]

At the beginning of October 1913 they met and Wittgenstein gave Russell a lengthy account of his work on logic. Fortunately, Russell had ordered a typist to be present, so Wittgenstein's summary survived and was eventually published in 1961 as *Notes on Logic*. The text formulates fundamental criticisms of Frege's and Russell's conception of the nature of logic, which were later incorporated in the *Tractatus*. *Notes on Logic* is the earliest philosophical text by Wittgenstein that has been preserved and it provides clear evidence that his primary interest at the time was the foundations of logic, and *not* ethics and mysticism, as it has become fashionable to claim. Ethics and mysticism were added only at a later stage, as we shall see, and any interpretation of the *Tractatus* must take this genealogy of his interests into account.

Despite this progress, Wittgenstein grew increasingly unhappy in Cambridge. His vacation breaks, whether on the Hochreit or in Norway, were more productive than his terms at the university. The distractions of the human comedy at Cambridge, which stimulated his morbid sensitivity and irritable disposition, were detrimental to the difficult intellectual work he needed to undertake. In addition, he believed that Russell had nothing to teach him any more and that there was nobody else from whom he could learn anything. So he decided to leave Cambridge for a longer period and work in solitude in Norway. Russell was not thrilled about this plan:

> my Austrian, Wittgenstein, burst in like a whirlwind, just back from Norway, and determined to return at once to live in complete solitude until he has solved *all* the problems of logic. I said it would be dark, and he said he hated daylight. I said it would be lonely, and he said he prostituted his mind talking to intelligent people. I said he was mad, and he said God preserve him from sanity. (God certainly will.)[27]

Wittgenstein's and Pinsent's postcard to William Eccles from Skjolden, Norway, 1913.

Russell eventually accepted this decision. Thus Wittgenstein's expensive furniture and a part of his belongings, including some of his papers, were put in storage and he said farewell to the great university that had hosted him for about two years. He left London in mid-October 1913, arrived in Bergen around three days later and soon settled in the small village of Skjolden, far away from any tourist routes and mundane distractions. Skjolden would become something of a second retreat for a good part of his life, and he returned there in times of inner turmoil and desire to work. Being far up in the north, close to the mountains and the glacier, the landscape was sober, almost grim, and had a quality of 'quiet seriousness', as he himself described it. His life in Skjolden was not entirely frugal and solitary: he lodged with the postmaster, Hans Klingenberg, who was an educated man and whose family took good care of Wittgenstein. He made several friends in the small community, for instance Arne Draegni, the son of a relatively wealthy family, whom he would visit to make music, and Anna Rebni, a local farmer. During his first year in Skjolden Wittgenstein learnt Norwegian and was able to read the works of writers like Ibsen in the original.

More importantly, he soon started to work, feeling that he had found his much-needed inspiration. He corresponded with both Russell and Frege on the foundations of logic. The letters he wrote to Frege have been lost, but their content can be partly inferred from Frege's surviving replies and Wittgenstein's subsequent writings. Those to Russell were equally important, for they contained not only his ideas about logic, but also formulated serious objections to Frege's views on language and thought. For instance, Frege held that every simple declarative sentence like 'Tom is American' has a sense and a reference. The sense is the thought expressed by the sentence, in our case the thought that Tom is American. Thoughts are not material objects; they do not have spatio-temporal and physical properties, but are 'abstract', like numbers. The reference is the truth-value of the sentence, 'The True' or 'The False', which are also abstract objects. Thus every true sentence refers to the object the True. But, as Wittgenstein noted, this commits the mistake of assimilating sentences to names, for it is the primary function of names to refer to objects. Sentences are very unlike names, be it only for the reason that you can negate a sentence, but not a name (what is 'not Charlie Chaplin' supposed to mean, taken by itself?). Wittgenstein also rejected Frege's account of intentionality, of the directedness of our thoughts and how they reach out to reality. Against Frege's claim that the sentence 'Tom believes that it is raining' signifies a relation between a person (Tom) and a thought ('It is raining'), Wittgenstein contended that when Tom thinks that it is raining, and it is indeed raining, then what Tom thinks is precisely what is the case, namely that it is raining. It is not true that there is a third entity, a thought, which is standing between Tom and reality, between Tom and what is the case. Rather, Tom's thought reaches right up to reality and is not an abstract object, as Frege believes. (Wittgenstein's theory is more complicated, since it purports to account for false sentences as well.)

On his way from Norway to Vienna Wittgenstein visited Frege in Jena for a few days and had several intensive discussions with him. The two philosophers did not come to an agreement on any substantial issue, but while his first visit in 1911 had ended with a feeling of defeat, Wittgenstein now believed that it was *he* who 'wiped the floor with Frege'.[28] They never met again. Nevertheless, Wittgenstein continued to admire Frege and always kept some of his writings with him, especially Frege's masterwork, *Basic Laws of Arithmetic*, from which he could recite whole passages by heart. In one of his last diary entries Wittgenstein wrote in 1951: 'Frege's style of writing is sometimes *great*; Freud writes excellently and it is a pleasure to read him, but his writing is never *great*.'[29]

After his Christmas vacation in Vienna, Wittgenstein returned to Skjolden and stayed there till June 1914. The problems of logic and language he was working on were very difficult and he felt he was making only very slow progress. His mood during these months seems to have been very dismal, verging on total despair, if not madness. During no other year did he spend more time con-templating suicide than in 1914. The circumstances were particularly severe. He was now not looking for approval from others any more, as he had done just two years before, but felt that he was expected, indeed that it was his calling, to solve the hardest problems of philosophy. Moreover, his brief stay in Vienna, where his family had commemorated his father's passing away the previous year (Karl had died of cancer in January 1913), deeply unsettled him and only added further to his inner torture. It was 'logic and sins' once again. We get a good sense of this double-edged pressure from his letters to Russell during this time:

> Sometimes things inside me are in such a ferment that I think
> I am going mad: then the next day I am totally apathetic again.
> But deep inside me there's a perpetual seething, like the bottom
> of a geyser, and I keep on hoping that things will come to an

eruption once and for all, so that I can turn into a different person. I can't write you anything about logic today. Perhaps you regard this thinking about myself as a waste of time – but how can I be a logician before I'm a human being! *Far* the most important thing is to settle accounts with myself![30]

It is VERY sad, but I have once again no logical news for you. The reason is that things have gone terribly badly for me in the last weeks. . . . Every day I was tormented by a frightful *Angst* and by depression in turns and even in the intervals I was so exhausted that I wasn't able to think of doing a bit of work. . . . I *never* knew what it meant to feel only one step away from madness.[31]

Ultimately, and remarkably, this state of mind was not counterproductive to his work. But it did affect his friendships with both Russell and Moore. The friendship with Russell received a blow from which it did not recover, while that with Moore suffered a serious setback and took many years to heal. We do not know exactly what happened between Wittgenstein and Russell but presumably early in 1914 Wittgenstein sent the latter a (lost) letter attempting to settle open issues in their relationship, including possibly Wittgenstein's dislike for Russell's libertarian lifestyle, but also differences in their attitude to scientific work. Russell seems to have been offended and his reaction, as he himself put it, was 'sharp'. A serious quarrel was the result, soon regretted by Russell, who asked Wittgenstein to lay the matter to rest. This was the right request to the wrong person:

But I can't possibly carry out your request . . . that would go clean contrary to my nature. . . . I have come to the conclusion that we really don't suit one another. *This is not meant as a reproach!* either for you or for me. But it is a fact. We've often had uncomfortable conversations with one another when certain subjects came up. . . . Our latest quarrel, too, was certainly not simply a result of your sensitiveness or my inconsiderateness. It came from deeper – from the fact that my letter must have shown you how totally different our ideas are, E.G. [*sic*] of the value of a scientific work. . . . I can see perfectly well that your value-judgements are just as good and just as deep-seated in you as mine in me, and that I have no right to catechize you. But I see equally clearly, now, that for that very reason there cannot be any real relation of friendship between us. *I shall be grateful to you and devoted to you with all my heart for the whole of my life, but I shall not write to you again and you will not see me again either.* Now that I am once again reconciled with you I want to part from you *in peace* . . . Goodbye![32]

Russell must have been taken aback by this letter. Nevertheless, he wrote Wittgenstein another conciliatory reply. The latter replied, thus breaking his resolution, but although his tone was now milder, Wittgenstein reaffirmed the differences between them. He suggested that they should never again speak about value-judgements, but only about objective matters, since he could not bear the hypocrisy of not being frank to a friend. Of course, it is not the best omen when friends start legislating which subjects they can discuss and which not. From early 1914 their relationship became one based on affection and respect, and their letters were mostly of a philosophical or at any rate not of an intimate kind.

The tension with Moore was of a different nature and entirely Wittgenstein's fault. Wittgenstein repeatedly urged Moore to come to Skjolden and work there, without realizing that the prospect of having to leave a comfortable academic environment in order to live in a remote Norwegian village while being exposed to Wittgenstein's overbearing presence might not tempt Moore. Indeed, Moore, a shy and sensitive man, was slightly afraid of Wittgenstein, especially after he heard about the quarrel with Russell. His reservations were eventually dropped and he visited Wittgenstein for two weeks in

March to April 1914. The stay was not without pleasant aspects, as they went on walks rich in stimulating conversations and played the piano with the Draegni family. But when it came to discussing philosophy and logic, Wittgenstein was entirely dominant, leaving to Moore the passive role of the audience. Moore made the best out of this role and wrote down most of what Wittgenstein said to him. These *Notes Dictated to G. E. Moore in Norway* comprise some fifteen pages and were published in 1961. Given how little else survives from Wittgenstein's earliest period, these dictations are of great value. They contain the earliest occurrence of the distinction between saying and showing, which is not only central to the *Tractatus* but has also gained some popularity outside of his philosophy, indeed outside of philosophy.

Upon his return to Cambridge Moore enquired with a university official whether it was possible for Wittgenstein, who was still nominally a 'research student', to submit his treatise on logic as a dissertation to obtain the BA degree. The answer was positive, but the condition was that the dissertation should fulfil the standard academic requirements, that is, contain a preface specifying what was original in the work and endnotes indicating the sources the author had used. Moore forwarded these requirements, which he had not stipulated, to Wittgenstein, who then became furious – not so much with the university as with Moore.

> Your letter annoyed me. When I wrote Logik [presumably a (lost) manuscript] I didn't consult the Regulations, and there-fore I think it would only be fair if you gave me my degree with-out consulting them so much either! As to a Preface and Notes; I think my examiners will easily see how much I have cribbed from Bosanquet. – If I am not worth your making an exception for me *even in some* STUPID *details* then I may as well go to Hell directly; and if I *am* worth it and you don't do it then – by God – you might go there.[33]

The hermit's retreat: Wittgenstein's house in Skjolden, Norway, built before the First World War.

Even if we take Wittgenstein's troubled state of mind into account, this letter was simply rude and unfair. Moore was deeply disturbed by it, as his diary entries show, and did not reply. Wittgenstein finally wrote to Moore again, sending him a half-hearted apology. Still, the friendship had received a heavy blow from which it recovered only when they met again fifteen years later.

After Moore's departure, Wittgenstein had a small wooden house built for him on the shores of a small lake a mile from Skjolden, planning to have a yet longer and even more secluded sojourn until he had solved the fundamental problems of logic. It is not clear whether he stayed in that house at all in 1914, as the furniture had not been brought in before he left Skjolden, but his desire to live in such ascetic circumstances says much about his tormented soul and the positive effect loneliness seemed to have on him. Other philosophers come to mind who chose to live in a hut far from the machinations of society, most notably Martin Heidegger and Constantin Noica.[34] But while in the case of Heidegger the hut was only the holiday retreat of a philosophy professor who otherwise lived in a comfortable villa in his hometown Freiburg, and thus mere bourgeois romanticism disguised as metaphysics, and in the case of Noica the seclusion was that of a passive dissident who cultivated his own philosophical school far away from the communist authorities, in Wittgenstein's case the seclusion was neither choice nor external constraint, but came out of inner necessity.

To avoid the impending tourist season, Wittgenstein left Norway in July 1914 for a visit home. He was not to return until 1921. Wittgenstein was at this moment a very wealthy man, since he had inherited, like his brother and sisters, a huge fortune from his father. His income amounted to at least £120,000 per year (translated into today's currency, and this might have been just the interest). But true to the charitable activities of his family, he sought ways of donating considerable amounts of it. As mentioned earlier, he was a keen reader of Karl Kraus's journal *Die Fackel*, indeed so keen that he had issues of it sent to Skjolden. It was in one of these issues that he had come across an article by Kraus on Ludwig von Ficker, a writer and editor of another Austrian literary journal, *Der Brenner*. In his typical satirical tone, Kraus wrote about *Der Brenner*: 'That Austria's only honest review is published in Innsbruck should be known, if not in Austria, at least in Germany, whose only honest review is also published in Innsbruck.'[35] It was, whether or not honest, a leading avant-garde journal, in which poets like Else Lasker-Schüler, Hermann Broch and Georg Trakl, probably the greatest expressionist poet of the German language, were publishing. The fact that Kraus admired Ficker gave Wittgenstein enough confidence to offer Ficker £40–50,000 for distribution among artists in need of it. Ficker was at first incredulous of this unexpected benefaction, but after a few letters were exchanged, he realized that Wittgenstein's intentions were genuine. They agreed that the beneficiaries should be Trakl, Lasker-Schüler, the painter Oskar Kokoschka, the architect Adolf Loos, the poets Theodor Däubler, Theodor Haecker, Rainer Maria Rilke and several others. Wittgenstein did not know the works of most of them. When Ficker sent him Trakl's poems, he commented: 'I do not understand them, but their *tone* makes me happy. It is the tone of true genius.' Remarkably, Wittgenstein almost met Trakl in 1914. While he was stationed in Krakow as an Austrian soldier, Wittgenstein learnt that Trakl, also an Austrian soldier, was in hospital there. He rushed to the hospital where Trakl was treated, but learnt, much to his consternation, that the poet had killed himself with an overdose of cocaine just three days before.

Wittgenstein did know and indeed appreciated Rilke's early work, which was written in a late nineteenth-century neo-Romantic style, and was moved by Rilke's letter of thanks:

> [It] both moved and deeply gladdened me. The affection of any noble human being is a support in the unsteady balance of my life. I am totally unworthy of the splendid present which I carry over my heart as a sign and remembrance of this affection. If you could only convey my deepest thanks and my faithful *devotion* to Rilke.[36]

He came, however, to disapprove of Rilke's great innovative works published after the First World War. Contemporary art and literature were, as mentioned, not to his liking. But there was one exception: architecture. Among the beneficiaries of his donation Adolf Loos was the only one whose art Wittgenstein really appreciated, although it was entirely progressive and modernistic. When Wittgenstein met Loos for the first time in a Viennese café through the mediation of von Ficker, the philosopher immediately engaged the architect, who was something of a controversial celebrity in the capital, in a heated discussion about modern architecture. But there was no deep-seated disagreement, since both had much in common, in particular an abhorrence of any kind of ornament. Loos had displayed his radical minimalism when erecting a much disputed building opposite the imperial palace, which was known as 'the house without eyebrows', because it lacked even dripstones above the windows.[37] For Loos this was not a purely stylistic choice, but expressed an ethical position as well. As a vehement opponent to Art Nouveau he wrote in his essay 'Ornament and Crime' (1908) that ornament was immoral and degenerate, the best sign that a civilization was decadent. Something is ornament when it is uselessly attached to a useful object, thus depriving art of its essence – a true 'crime'. 'The evolution of culture is synonymous with the elimination of ornament from objects of daily use.'[38] We can see how this austere minimalism appealed to Wittgenstein's ideal of purity as a quality he had found so appealing in Weininger's writings. Loos soon became a reference point for Wittgenstein and was to influence his own architectural endeavours when he helped build a mansion for his sister Margarete in the 1920s. However, after the war he came to dislike Loos, because in his eyes Loos had become infected with 'virulent bogus intellectualism'. This pattern of attraction and disaffection, of interest and disappointment, characterized many of Wittgenstein's relationships; if the person in question was not up to his standards, ethical or otherwise, he was simply not able to meet them any more. Wittgenstein had to accept their entire personality or discontinue the friendship.

3

In the Trenches, 1914–18

On 28 July 1914 Austria declared war on Serbia. Although not liable
to military service owing to a hernia, Wittgenstein volunteered for
service on 7 August. Two days later he started work on the earliest
surviving manuscript of the *Tractatus*, the manuscript that is now
classified as MS 101 (published in *Notebooks, 1914–1916*). Throughout
the war he continued working on philosophy. His method of work,
then as later, was to enter insights into notebooks in the form of separate but related remarks. These were sometimes no more than a sentence or two of highly condensed reflection, the trajectory of which
was indicated but not elaborated. At least five more manuscripts were
to follow before he considered this book completed in the summer of
1918. The *Tractatus* was thus entirely composed during the war, while
its author was serving at the front, at times in the trenches, in the
middle of dreadful battles. The experience of war left its mark on the
author and his book. His work on the foundations of logic and language was not affected, but the last pages of the *Tractatus* deal with
ethics and mysticism, topics that he approached later in the war.

Wittgenstein enlisted out of the patriotic feeling that he needed
to defend his country but, unlike most of his countrymen, he did
not share the enthusiasm about the war that drove millions to
senseless death. He wrote in his diary:

[It] seems to me as good as certain that we cannot get the upper
hand against England. The English – the best race in the world

– *cannot* lose. We, however, can lose and shall lose, if not this
year, then next year. The thought that our race is going to be
beaten depresses me terribly, because I am completely German.[1]

Patriotism aside, the other reason for going to war was a feeling
typical of others as well, especially for intellectuals: the feeling that
Europe was decadent and dead, that one had to do something real,
reconnect to 'life'. As his sister Hermine explains in her memoirs,
Wittgenstein 'had the intense wish to assume some heavy burden
and to perform some task other than purely intellectual work'.
He viewed the war, like other contemporaries, as a personal test,
believing he would only discover his worth by facing death.

Wittgenstein got a first taste of the war very soon. Initially
assigned to an artillery regiment, he was, ten days after his enlist-
ment, transferred to a small gunboat, the *Goplana*, which ventured
down the Vistula river into enemy territory. Here is his account of the
first assignment, in his nightwear, a day after his arrival on the boat:

> Suddenly woke about 1 a.m. Called for by the Lieutenant who
> says I must go to the searchlight straightaway: 'no getting
> dressed'. I ran to the bridge almost naked. Icy wind, rain.
> I was certain I was going to die on the spot. . . . I was *frightfully*
> agitated and groaned audibly. I felt the terrors of war. Now
> (in the evening) I have got over the terror. Unless I change my
> present bent of mind I'll strive with all my might to stay alive.[2]

The task of manning the searchlight was that of a private and relatively dangerous. The real problem, however, was his shipmates,
and later his comrades at the Eastern front, whom he found
unbearable. With a few exceptions they were, from his point of
view, 'a company of drunkards, a company of vile and stupid people',
'malicious and heartless', '*appallingly* limited', indeed lacking
humanity, as he wrote in his diary in the spring of 1916. Most of

them were working-class men with whom Wittgenstein had little in common. But the life on a crammed ship in a limiting situation brought out the differences between them and him much more strongly. He felt hated by them and in turn hated them. His manners and mannerisms, his fastidiousness and refinement were only a liability in these circumstances, especially as these distinctive features did not correlate with higher rank. As in the school in Linz, he felt ostracized and betrayed. He tried repeatedly to exercise Christian humility, urging himself to understand and tolerate his comrades. But even when the hatred was overcome, his disgust persisted. Nevertheless, and this was a typical Wittgensteinian self-torture, he did not seek relief from this situation; although he was entitled to certain privileges having graduated in Linz, Wittgenstein refused to make use of them for a prolonged period.

Wittgenstein was caught up in the ill-fated Eastern campaign of 1914, which came to a halt, if not retreat, in early November, and his diary gives an accurate depiction of disintegrating Austrian morale. It also gives us, through encoded notations, an invaluable insight into his philosophical progress, and into more intimate matters. We also get an understanding of his general state of mind, the phases of heavy depression interspersed with almost mystical outbursts. These were a novelty, since Wittgenstein was not religious before the war, having lost his childhood faith in Linz. The war changed him. It is hard to say whether we can speak of a proper conversion. But it would be certainly wrong to describe him as non-religious after August 1914. It was some time early in his service that he went into a bookstore in Tarnow, discovering that apart from postcards it contained only one book: Tolstoy's *Gospel in Brief*. He bought it, read and re-read it, and kept it on him at all times (which earned him the byword 'the one with the Gospels' from his comrades). As McGuinness sees it, Wittgenstein found in Tolstoy's version of Christianity a path to happiness that seemed to suit his wretched situation in the army, if not even his earlier

Wittgenstein's military identity card.

misery, for it offered a recipe for becoming independent of externally induced humiliation and suffering: to be saved from death, one must renounce one's selfish instincts and become one with the spirit that unites us all in God. One must live a life in the service of others, immortalize oneself by fighting against the egoistic nature that is the true source of all suffering. Tolstoy certainly provided him with consolation:

> The news gets worse and worse. Tonight there will be instant readiness. I work every day, more or less, and with fair confidence. I say Tolstoy's words again and again in my head. 'Man is powerless in the flesh but free because of the spirit.' May the spirit be in me! . . . How will I behave when it comes to shooting? I am not afraid of being shot but of not doing my duty properly. God give me strength! Amen. Amen. Amen.[3]

He wrote a day later: 'Now I may have the opportunity to be a decent human being, because I am face to face with death.' No doubt a religious voice is speaking here, but it is Christian only in so far as it is mediated through Tolstoy's interpretation. After all, Wittgenstein's prayers were brief and invoked the 'spirit', not Jesus. Was this not rather an intellectual's rationalized version of religion, a refined version of the 'duty to oneself' urged by Weininger? Not so much a real belief in Jesus' teachings, his crucifixion and the mystery of his resurrection, but the acceptance of Tolstoyan inwardness as the best recipe to cope with serious existential difficulties? Such a 'streamlined' form of religion had its own tradition in Western thought, having precursors in David Friedrich Strauss, Schopenhauer and Ralph Waldo Emerson (the latter two read by Wittgenstein during the war as well). These are difficult questions. In any case, he felt Christian enough to be troubled by Nietzsche's *The Anti-Christ*, a book he read towards the end of 1914:

> I am strongly affected by [Nietzsche's] hostility against Christianity. Because his writings too have some truth in them. To be sure, Christianity is the only *sure* way to happiness; but what if someone spurned this happiness? Might it not be better to perish unhappily in the hopeless struggle against the external world? But such a life is senseless. . . . what must I do in order that my life shall not be lost to me? I must be conscious of it all the time.[4]

Questions about life and death were of *personal* not philosophical concern to Wittgenstein at this time, and the coded diary entries about them stand next to his extensive, but unrelated and not coded, notes on the foundations of logic, language and ontology. This needs to be stressed to counter those exaggerated if fashionable interpretations that claim that his ethical and his logical concerns were two sides of the same coin. When he came under enemy fire or plunged into the immense suffering of his inner abyss, Wittgenstein did not seek salvation through the solution of Russell's Paradox and did not pray to the Muse of Logic or the Great Quantifier, but to the God of Tolstoy's *Gospel*. To claim some kind of unity between his logical investigations and his religious problems is to romanticize the former and trivialize the latter.

Wittgenstein spent 1915 in relative safety in an artillery workshop in Krakow, where his skills as an engineer were much relied upon. In the summer he suffered a minor injury from an explosion in the workshop and had to spend some time in hospital. He then returned to another artillery shop, located on board a train close to Lvov. Finally, at his own request, he was transferred to a howitzer regiment on the Russian front in Galicia in March 1916. Here he volunteered for service at the artillery observation post at night, the place and time of maximal risk. McGuinness describes this phase as 'one of the hardest times of his life' and this is not exaggerated.[5] Wittgenstein contracted food-poisoning and other illnesses, felt ostracized by his comrades and, finally, towards the end of April experienced his first combat situation at an observation-post where he came under direct fire. Nevertheless, he felt that he would commit suicide if he were to be sent away. 'Perhaps nearness to death will bring light into my life.'[6] There is something moving and inspiring in the way Wittgenstein exhorts himself in this period of grave danger. Despite what his sister Hermine believed at times, he was certainly not a saint. But there is a disarming authenticity in his diary entries, an authenticity that many of those who met him have observed. In the midst of battles he finds consolation in prayers, in soliloquies with himself and God. 'My soul shrivels up. God give me light! God give me light! God give light to my soul!'[7] 'God is all that man needs.'[8] How different is this man from the arrogant student in Cambridge, who, in Russell's own words, was more terrible with Christians than Russell himself!

> Do your best. You cannot do more. And be cheerful. Be content with yourself. Because others will not prop you up or at most

only for a short time (then you will become burdensome to them). Help yourself and help others with your strength. And at the same time be cheerful. But how much strength ought one to use for oneself and how much for others? It is difficult to live a good life. But the good life is something fine. Yet not my will but thine be done.[9]

It was only after spending several months under the most dangerous circumstances that these personal notes began to connect with the philosophical system he was developing, in the form of uncoded *general* remarks about God, ethics and the meaning of life, some of which made it into the last pages of the *Tractatus*. They reflect not only his recent experiences, but also his readings of Schopenhauer, Nietzsche, Emerson, Tolstoy, Dostoevsky (he read *The Brothers Karamazov* so many times that he knew whole passages from it by heart). Here is a sample of these powerful remarks:

What do I know about God and the purpose of life? – I know that this world exists. – That I am placed in it like my eyes in its visual field. – That something about it is problematic, which we call its meaning. – That this meaning does not lie in it but outside it. – That life is the world. – That my will is good or evil. – Therefore that good and evil are somehow connected with the meaning of the world. – The meaning of life, i.e. the meaning of the world, we can call God.[10]

Death is not an event in life. It is not a fact of the world. – If by eternity is understood not infinite temporal duration but non-temporality, then it can be said that a man lives eternally if he lives in the present. – In order to live happily I must be in agreement with the world. And that is what 'being happy' *means*. – I am then, so to speak, in agreement with that alien will on which I appear dependent. That is to say: 'I am doing the will of God'. –

Fear in face of death is the best sign of a false, i.e. – a bad, life.[11]

When a general ethical law of the form 'Thou shalt . . .' is set up, the first thought is: Suppose I do not do it? – But it is clear that ethics has nothing to do with punishment and reward. So this question about the consequences of an action must be unimportant. At least these consequences cannot be events. For there must be something right about the question after all. There must be a *kind* of ethical reward and of ethical punishment but these must be involved in the action itself. – And it is also clear that the reward must be something pleasant, the punishment something unpleasant. – I keep on coming back to this! simply the happy life is good, the unhappy bad. And if I *now* ask myself: But why should I live *happily*, then this of itself seems to me to be a tautological question; the happy life seems to be justified, of itself, it seems that it *is* the only right life. – But this is really in some sense deeply mysterious! *It is clear* that ethics *cannot* be expressed![12]

We find in these remarks several interconnected themes. One is about human happiness: it is achieved only through good deeds and in these good deeds. Happiness cannot be achieved if understood as an external goal. Related to this is a Stoic attitude of not being affected by any event in the world, especially life-threatening events. Another related theme is moral solipsism, the view that good and evil are not in the world, but given through *me*, *my* perspective on the entire world. Finally, there is the contention that ethics is 'transcendental', that the most important values in human life, the Good, happiness, God, all things he summarized by the term 'the Higher', are not part of this world, nothing that one could find or discover through a scientific observation of the physical realm. Values are given through an attitude towards the entire world, and thus cannot be part of the world. But since all that can be expressed, that is, the real objects in the world and their properties, must be expressible in terms of scientific language, it follows that the content of ethics cannot be expressed. It can only be shown. We encounter here the distinction between what can be said and what only shown that is crucial for his logical and metaphysical doctrines as well, as we will see. But, we may already ask, has Wittgenstein himself not just told us, at least to some extent, what ethics consist in? Has he not just said that values are not part of this world, that the good deed finds reward in itself etc., indeed that ethics is that very thing about which one cannot talk? There is something paradoxical about this saying/showing distinction, as applied to his views on ethics and those on logic and metaphysics.

Wittgenstein was aware that the scope of his investigation had widened. As he put it towards the end of the summer of 1916: 'My work has extended from the foundations of logic to the nature of the world.'[13] His diary entries in this period are much more sparse than before, but it remains an amazing fact that he managed to do any philosophy under the given circumstances. For this was no ordinary summer. His division had been caught up in the Russian Brusilov offensive and forced to retreat with very heavy losses (around 80 per cent, according to some calculations). His division then fought in the Bukovina and in the battle of Kolomea. His conduct during the fighting was exemplary, as we know from reports by his officers. One such report states that 'Ignoring the heavy artillery fire on the casemate and the exploding mortar bombs [Wittgenstein] observed the discharge of the mortars and located them. . . . By this distinctive behaviour he exercised a very calming effect on his comrades.'[14] He received two medals and was promoted to the rank of corporal.

Owing to his conduct at the front Wittgenstein was sent to an officers' school in Olmütz, Moravia, in October 1916. Here he met Paul Engelmann, a young Jewish architect, pupil of Loos and friend of Kraus, who shared much of Wittgenstein's artistic outlook and occasionally published in *Die Fackel*. They soon became close friends. It was a remarkable friendship, which lasted for well over a decade and would eventually lead to their cooperation on building the famous mansion for Margarete Wittgenstein in the late 1920s.

In Olmütz Wittgenstein started to participate in Engelmann's literary circle, made up mostly of cultivated young Jews, literati, artists, etc. He immediately became the centre point of the circle, indeed something of a star. He was member of a famous Viennese family, had a refined sense of culture, had studied philosophy and logic with Russell in Cambridge, was developing his own philosophical system and, last but not least, had just returned from the Eastern front, where he had been face to face with death. The members of the circle staged *A Midsummer Night's Dream* and Molière's *Le Malade imaginaire*; they read classic German poets such as Goethe and Schiller (on one of these occasions Wittgenstein praised Schiller's love for freedom); they performed *Salonmusik*, for instance by Schubert and Brahms; they engaged in conversations about ethics, aesthetics and authors dear to Wittgenstein, such as Schopenhauer, Tolstoy, Dostoevsky and Weininger; and they read the New Testament together. Wittgenstein even made them read some Frege and he explained his philosophical system to Engelmann. Compared to the moral and existential morass of the Front these encounters were bliss. But Olmütz provided him not only with relaxation for his battered soul; this encounter with a select group of intellectuals led also to a heightened interest for questions of aesthetics, reflections on which resurfaced in the *Tractatus*. It was here that he finally managed to make a connection between logic, ethics and aesthetics, and thus confirm Weininger's idea that all three were one and the same, an idea that actually goes back to antiquity.[15] He wrote in his diary: 'The work of art is the object seen *sub specie aeternitatis* and the good life is the world seen *sub specie aeternitatis*. This is the connection between art and ethics.'[16]

The encounter with the Olmütz circle can be seen as noteworthy in another respect: it was Wittgenstein's only encounter with a Jewish environment. But the Jewishness of these young men was not very substantial. What connected both parties was 'the need for a self-made religion'.[17] As McGuinness sees it, Wittgenstein was looking for a substitute for his traditional Christian upbringing, while the Olmütz intellectuals were looking for an alternative to a Jewishness that had lost its traditional meaning.[18]

In January 1917 Wittgenstein returned to the Eastern front as an officer. He had just donated 1 million crowns to the Austrian government for the development of a 12-inch howitzer. He was soon involved in heavy fighting again, in the Kerensky Offensive, awarded another medal for gallantry and recommended for further promotion. In February 1918 he was promoted to lieutenant, and in March he was transferred to the Italian front. In the Austrian June offensive he behaved with outstanding courage and saved the lives of several comrades. He was recommended for the gold medal for valour (the Austrian equivalent of the Victoria Cross), but was eventually awarded a slightly lesser distinction. In a report about him we read: 'His exceptionally courageous behaviour, calmness, sang-froid, and heroism won the total admiration of the troops. By his conduct he gave a splendid example of loyal and soldierly fulfilment of duty.'[19]

The year 1918 was important for Wittgenstein in several respects. First, the war came to an end, for him in fact a week earlier than the final Armistice, since he was taken prisoner by the Italians near Trento. Second, it was the year in which he lost his dear friend David Pinsent. Pinsent had not been called up for active duty during the war, but had trained as a test pilot. He crashed with his plane on a test flight in May 1918. This was a grave loss for Wittgenstein and may explain his subsequent plan to kill himself while on leave in Austria. There is some indication that his uncle Paul Wittgenstein saved his life. Paul, an estate manager, painter and patron of the arts, who had a weakness for his nephew, bumped into Ludwig at Salzburg train station when Ludwig was contemplating suicide.[20] Pinsent and Wittgenstein had exchanged letters during the war (via Switzerland) and Pinsent's letters were a great source of comfort. When he received Pinsent's first war letter in 1914, Wittgenstein kissed it out of excitement. He had a great desire to see his friend again, addressing him as 'My *dear* Davy' and writing in his diary 'Lovely letter from David. . . . Answered David. *Very* sensual.'[21] These passages suggest that Ludwig may indeed have felt unrequited love for David, a fact of which he was not unaware, writing in his diary: 'I wonder whether he thinks of me half as much as I think of him.'

Last but not least, 1918 was also the year in which Wittgenstein completed his book, the *Tractatus Logico-Philosophicus*. He dedicated it to David Pinsent.

4

Logic and Mysticism: The *Tractatus*

The *Tractatus* was the fruit of six years of intense labour and the only philosophical book published in Wittgenstein's lifetime. He initially called it *Logisch-philosophische Abhandlung* and it was only later that the English translation received, on Moore's suggestion, the Latin title *Tractatus Logico-Philosophicus*, by which it is known today. How the book was finally put together is not fully documented. As mentioned, in the period 1914–18 he filled several notebooks, which he then unified in a single manuscript. The last manuscript (MS 104) is the most important one, as it largely prefigures the actual book, save the ordering of its proposition and the Preface. Now known as the *Prototractatus*, it was published in 1971. The *Tractatus* is a unique book in the history of philosophy, if only because of its style. It is short, around 90 pages in the English translation. It consists of the following seven main propositions:

1. The world is everything that is the case.
2. What is the case, the fact, is the existence of atomic facts.
3. The logical picture of the facts is the thought.
4. The thought is the significant proposition.
5. Propositions are truth-functions of elementary propositions. (An elementary proposition is a truth-function of itself.)
6. The general form of truth-function is: $[\bar{p}, \bar{\xi}, N(\bar{\xi})]$. This is the general form of proposition.
7. Whereof one cannot speak, thereof one must be silent.

Each of these propositions, apart from the last one, is further explained by other numbered entries, and so on. For instance, proposition 1 is explained by 1.1 ('The world is the totality of facts, not things'), which in turn is explained by two further propositions, 1.11 and 1.12. This gives the book the impression of a precisely structured investigation, almost like a mathematical proof, and indeed the numbered propositions bear some similarity to the proofs in the *Principia Mathematica*. Probably the only other book in European philosophy that surpasses its aspiration to mathematical beauty and simplicity is Spinoza's *Ethics* (1677), which has definitions, axioms and lemmas, just like an actual mathematical proof. But the *Tractatus* is probably more difficult to understand, not least because it is dense with the technical terminology and formalism of modern mathematical logic, which is not penetrable without familiarity with the logic of Frege and Russell. Also, Wittgenstein, unlike Spinoza, does not define many of his key notions and does not indicate how he has arrived at his propositions. The readers are left to figure out for themselves what these propositions mean and what the arguments leading to them consist of. We would have probably been at a loss if none of his notebooks had survived.

The understanding of the book is further complicated by the fact that in composing it Wittgenstein followed a certain *aesthetic* ideal. It is certainly not true, as some interpreters have suggested, that the *Tractatus* must be seen as a work of art, a 'poem'.[1] And it is not correct, as Terry Eagleton has it, that the 'true coordinates' of the *Tractatus* are really Joyce, Schönberg and Picasso, and not Frege and Russell.[2] The true coordinates of the book *are* Frege and Russell, and their investigations into the nature of logic. It contains a complex philosophical system, based on predominantly implicit arguments, but arguments nevertheless. But it is true that there is a strongly artistic side to the book. Wittgenstein was always drawn to writing fragments and aphorisms, partly through the influence of Schopenhauer and Lichtenberg, and this explains the fragmentary character of many of his writings. In addition, he was attracted to Loos's and Weininger's ideal of purity and minimalism, an ideal that, as discussed earlier, denounced any ornament as a 'crime'. In the Preface Wittgenstein writes: 'If this work has any value, it consists in . . . [the fact] that thoughts are expressed in it, and on this score the better the thoughts are expressed – the more the nail has been hit on the head – the greater will be its value.' Wittgenstein subjected his philosophical prose to the perfectionist ideal of finding the most precise expression, 'the liberating word'[3] that would be 'setting the carriage precisely on the rails'.[4] He looked at his writing with the eyes of a poet; no word or sentence should be superfluous or casual. 'I think I summed up my attitude to philosophy when I said: philosophy ought really to be written only as a poetic composition.'[5] He wrote this around 1933, but it is representative of his lifelong attitude to the composition of philosophical texts. This attitude was particularly extreme with respect to the *Tractatus*. For in this book Wittgenstein sought to eliminate any redundancy by keeping his prose condensed to a bare minimum. Many propositions of the *Tractatus* exhibit therefore the character of definitive oracular pronouncements. As he self-critically acknowledged later, '[e]very sentence in the *Tractatus* should be seen as the heading of a chapter needing further exposition'.[6] Wittgenstein was not interested in writing a book for an academic audience, but in reaching a kind of crystalline beauty. We find confirmation of this self-imposed aesthetic requirement in an early report by Russell:

I told him he ought not simply to *state* what he thinks true, but to give arguments for it, but he said arguments spoil its beauty, and that he would feel as if he was dirtying a flower with muddy hands. I told him I hadn't the heart to say anything against that, and that he had better acquire a slave to state the arguments. I am seriously afraid that no one will see the point of anything he writes, because he won't recommend it by arguments addressed to a different point of view.[7]

What is now the content of the *Tractatus*? A detailed answer would be the subject of a long monograph, but the general idea of the book is not too difficult to sketch. The *Tractatus* is a breathtakingly ambitious book. Above all, it claims to give the definitive account of the nature of philosophy and the final solution of the problems of philosophy. In particular, it offers an account of the essence of language (logic), the world (ontology) and their relation (intentionality). It also attempts to clarify the status of mathematics and scientific theories, reconciles solipsism with realism, denounces scepticism, and determines the nature of aesthetics, ethics and mysticism.

The *Tractatus*'s account of language is the core topic of the book, with the ontology giving it the metaphysical underpinning. Wittgenstein's ontology is atomistic, like Russell's. The world is composed of basic, simple elements that cannot be divided further. They are not the atoms of the physicists, but something more abstract. In Wittgenstein's case they are so-called atomic or *elementary facts*. That the broom is standing in the corner is a fact, for instance. However, this fact is not an elementary one, but rather compound; it can be divided further, that is, into the fact that the broomstick and the brush are standing in certain spatial relations to each other and the fact that the broomstick and the brush are standing in certain spatial relations to the corner, etc. What then is an example of an elementary fact? Wittgenstein does not tell us, since his task at this stage is wholly programmatic. All that he tells us is that each elementary fact is not further divisible and obtains independently of any other facts.

Thus one aspect of Wittgenstein's atomism concerns facts. The other concerns objects. After all, what makes a fact is that objects are related to each other in a certain way, for example, the broomstick and the brush. Just as there are elementary facts there are also atomic objects, which are not further divisible. Save for some uncertain examples, such as the smallest visible spot in the visual field, Wittgenstein does not indicate what these atomic objects might be. Again, we are only given a general description: for example, that an elementary fact consists of certain atomic objects being related to each other in a certain way, or that ordinary physical objects are not atomic objects, but composed out of atomic objects. Of course, facts may come and go, but the atomic objects remain just the same. They can occur in various different facts, but they are indestructible, since they are not further divisible. They are what Wittgenstein calls 'the substance of the world' – that of which everything there is consists. Every atomic object has a metaphysical essence. What is it? It is the totality of all facts in which it can occur. This may sound mysterious, but it is not really. For instance, the metaphysical essence of the broomstick (assuming, to illustrate, that it is an atomic object) consists of all the possible facts of which it might be a part. For it is part of the broomstick's essence not only that it is stuck into the brush, as it actually is, but also that it could be lying on the left of the brush, on the right of it, on top of it, etc. All these possibilities are already inscribed into the inner essence of the broomstick and thus fully determine its nature. Imagine we have a list of all atomic objects in the world. In that case we would be able to determine any possible course of the world, that is, every possible fact, everything that might be the case – all possible worlds. No possibility could ever be surprising in this glacial and crystalline Tractarian world.

Wittgenstein had initially given his treatise the working title 'Der Satz' ('The proposition' or 'The sentence'), a clear proof that the nature of propositions occupies the centre stage of the book. Wittgenstein's focus on propositions, that is, declarative statements like 'Ronaldo is a football player' or 'The moon is 239,000 miles away from Earth', is not arbitrary. For the main function of language is to describe the world, and propositions are the smallest units of communication. His theory of proposition consists of two

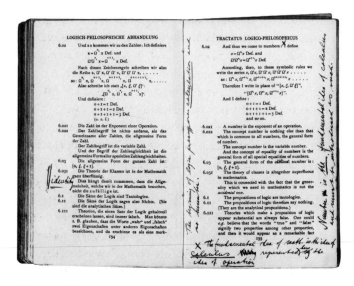

Wittgenstein's annotated bilingual edition of *Tractatus*.

aspects. The first aspect can be summarized by the label 'logical atomism'. Atomism applies to propositions as much as it applies to facts. There are complex propositions, such as 'Ronaldo is a Brazilian football player AND Maradona is an Argentinian football player', and they consist of elementary (or atomic) propositions, in our case of 'Ronaldo is a Brazilian football player' and 'Maradona is an Argentinian football player'. Elementary propositions are elementary in a similar way in which elementary facts are elementary: they are true or false independently of whether any other elementary proposition is true or false. Note, however, that the sentences just mentioned are only illustrations, not really examples of elementary propositions. But what is then an example of an elementary proposition? Again, Wittgenstein does not tell us, since his approach is purely programmatic.

The second aspect of his theory can be summarized by the label 'picture theory of proposition'. Propositions are pictures.

Every proposition is a description of a possible fact. Giving an account of what a proposition is, what makes it meaningful and how it manages to describe a fact, is of pivotal importance for understanding how any discourse about the world, and in particular scientific discourse, is possible. Legend has it that Wittgenstein thought of the picture theory when he read in a newspaper about a Parisian trial in which toys were used to depict a car accident. For example, one could use a blue toy car to depict a real blue car and a red toy bus to depict a real bus. In addition, one could draw an intersection on a paper depicting the real intersection and then place the toy cars in a way that depicts the way the real cars were related to each other. Wittgenstein took this to be the essence of pictures in general and of linguistic pictures, that is, propositions, in particular. The elements of a picture stand for the objects they depict, and the way the elements are ordered in the picture mirrors the depicted fact. Similarly, the elements of a proposition, the words, stand for the objects they depict. A proposition is true if the expressions contained in it are arranged in a way similar to the way in which the objects for which they stand are arranged. To give a very simplified example: the proposition 'Ronaldo is standing left of Maradona' is true in a situation in which Ronaldo is standing left of Maradona, since the name 'Ronaldo' is also standing left of the name 'Maradona'. The connection between language and reality is established via private mental acts of meaning by a given word '*w*', the object '*w*' is meant to stand for. It follows that the meaning of every word is the object it stands for, and thus that every word is the *name* of an object. If a word does not stand for an object, it is meaningless. Propositions, we can conclude, consist of names, and if a proposition contains at least one meaningless word, then the proposition is meaningless as well. This is how we can visualize the picture theory:

LANGUAGE		WORLD
True propositions	describe	Facts
consist of		consist of configurations of
Names	stand for	Objects

We see that language and the world are intimately connected. Propositions are supposed to consist solely of names. This does not sound very plausible, since there seem to be so many propositions that do not even contain names, for example, 'It is raining' or 'All monkeys sleep too much'. But this is not a problem for Wittgenstein, since for him, as for Russell, the real structure of language cannot be read off the surface of the ordinary sentences we usually utter. To find out the real structure of our propositions we must employ logical analysis. All languages have the same deep structure, which we can uncover by formal logic. This is an idea that became very dominant not only in analytic philosophy but also in linguistics, for example, via Noam Chomsky's theories of generative grammar after the Second World War.

There is a further important aspect of Wittgenstein's theory. Since a proposition is a picture, it is meaningful insofar as it describes a possible fact. The fact does not have to obtain; it is contingent. If a fact obtains, it is intelligible to assume that it might not have obtained, and if does not obtain, it is intelligible to assume that it might have obtained. For instance, if this table is brown, then the possibility that it could be green is still intelligible. Indeed, it must be intelligible if the proposition 'This table is brown' is to be meaningful and have a sense. In short: a proposition is meaningful only if it depicts a fact that *could* be otherwise, only if the proposition is capable of being true *and* capable of being false. (The only exception to this rule are the propositions of logic, i.e. tautologies such as 'Either it is raining or it is not raining', which, given that they are necessarily true, cannot be false even in principle.)

This aspect of Wittgenstein's theory of proposition has dramatic consequences, not least for his own theory. For it means that a proposition that tries to depict some non-contingent fact, for example a 'metaphysical fact', which could not be otherwise, is simply meaningless. Any proposition whose negation is inconceivable is of this kind. Take for instance the statement 'Red is a colour'. Could red not be a colour? What would this mean? How could we find out that red is not a colour? This seems to be a sheer impossibility. Or take 'This table is an object'. Sentences of this kind only look like genuine propositions, but are in fact pseudo-propositions. It follows that all the metaphysical propositions of traditional philosophy, for example Spinoza's theory about the identity of God with nature or Schopenhauer's claim that the world is the product of will, are meaningless. Equally, Russell's statements about the essence of the world that he needed in order to defend his logic turn out to be without meaning. And last, but not least, the propositions of the *Tractatus* themselves prove now to be totally meaningless, indeed pure nonsense! For is it not the case that they are trying to describe the metaphysical, unchangeable essence of the world and of language? Indeed, this is what they are trying to do. Take the first proposition of the *Tractatus*, 'The world is everything that is the case', and assume that it is true. For it to be meaningful, according to the picture theory, this proposition must depict a contingent fact. It should be at least intelligible to imagine that the world is *not* everything that is the case. But this is precisely what is not possible, since the proposition does attempt to describe a non-contingent, essential feature of the world. The ontological propositions of the *Tractatus* thus turn out to be nonsensical (not: false). The semantic theory of the book does not fare better. Take

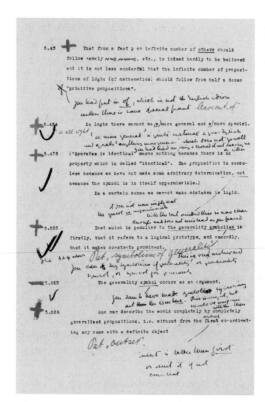

A page of Wittgenstein's annotations to the typescript of the English translation of the *Tractatus*.

the proposition 'A proposition is a picture of reality' (*Tractatus* 4.01). Does this describe a contingent fact, which could be otherwise? It certainly does not, at least not according to the *Tractatus*. Rather, it describes an essential feature of any proposition whatsoever, a feature no proposition could ever lack without becoming meaningless. Thus proposition 4.01 falls under Wittgenstein's own nonsense verdict: it fails to describe a contingent fact and is thus meaningless. And so do almost all other propositions in his book. They try to say something that cannot be put in words. They are pseudo-propositions. As Frank Ramsey (1903–1930), one of the earliest reviewers of the *Tractatus* and later a friend of Wittgenstein, expressed it, 'What we can't say we can't say, and we can't whistle it either' (a humorous hint to Wittgenstein's remarkable ability to whistle any tune).

Wittgenstein helps himself out of this impasse by making a distinction between what can be said, that is, contingent facts about the world, which are the subject matter of science, and what cannot be said, but shows itself – the metaphysical essence of language and the world. This is the actual justification of the famous distinction between *saying* and *showing*. It follows that there are no philosophical propositions, no philosophical claims that can be expressed. All deep truths can only be shown. Philosophy is not a science and not in competition with science, offering doctrines and hypotheses about the world, whether empirically testable or justified through *a priori* reasoning. It does not add to the sum of human knowledge. Rather, philosophy is a discipline in its own right, 'above or below the natural sciences, not beside them' (*Tractatus* 4.111). It is an activity, and to a large degree a critical one, namely the clarification of language by means of logical analysis.

> The correct method in philosophy would really be the following: to say nothing except what can be said, i.e. propositions of natural science – i.e. something that has nothing to do with philosophy – and then, whenever someone else wanted to say something metaphysical, to demonstrate to him that he had failed to give a meaning to certain signs in his propositions. Although it would not be satisfying to the other person – he would not have the feeling that we were teaching him philosophy – this method would be the only strictly correct one [*Tractatus* 6.53].

The conception of philosophy intimated here was radical and new at the time. It marks what has come to be known as the *linguistic turn*, a paradigm change that, Wittgenstein thought, finally gave philosophy the rigorous method philosophers had always been looking for. Unlike his predecessors, Wittgenstein envisaged this method to consist of the analysis of language, not the world. The sole task for future philosophy is to monitor the bounds of sense in order to delimit science from the nonsense of metaphysics, namely by elucidating the hidden logical forms of philosophically problematic sentences. Some aspects of this linguistic turn had been formulated by Frege and Russell as well, but it was really the *Tractatus* that heralded this paradigm change in an explicit manner. It was a paradigm that remained very influential in philosophy, at least in the Anglophone world, until the 1970s.

The philosophy of the *Tractatus* can be seen as defending science against metaphysics. Nevertheless, the book itself is highly metaphysical, indeed mystical. It delimits what can be genuinely said, namely by means of science, from what cannot, but the latter is not a chimera. There *are* deep metaphysical truths, although they are strictly ineffable and can only be shown, indeed felt. In a line reminiscent of certain mystics Wittgenstein writes: 'To view the world sub *specie aeterni* is to view it as a whole – a limited whole. Feeling the world as a limited whole – it is this that is mystical' (*Tractatus* 6.45). Linguistic analysis is not meant to deny these truths, but make room for them, in other words make room for metaphysics, ethics, aesthetics, God, in short for all that which Wittgenstein subsumes under the label 'the Higher'. Thus we do find remarks about the Higher at the end of the *Tractatus*. We can speak only about what is *in* the world, for example, the World Cup of 2006, stockmarkets, 9/11, climate change, social policy, molecular genetics, the solar system, etc. But '[h]ow things are in the world is a matter of complete indifference for what is the Higher. God does not reveal himself in the world' (*Tractatus* 6.432). It is in this context that Wittgenstein presents several of his remarks on ethics and the meaning of life he wrote in the trenches in 1916. The meaning of life, the primary subject of ethics, is radically transcendent and cannot be expressed. The most important things are ineffable. 'We feel that even when all possible scientific questions have been answered, the problems of life remain completely untouched. Of course there are then no questions left, and this itself is the answer' (*Tractatus* 6.52). 'There are, indeed, things that cannot be put into words. They make themselves manifest. They are what is mystical' (*Tractatus* 6.522). Thence the famous concluding remark that what we cannot speak about we must pass over in silence. Ironically, it is this remark and the previous ones on ethics that have generated a massive secondary literature. But if we are to take Wittgenstein seriously, then silence should mean silence. As he explained to Ludwig von Ficker in a letter from October 1919,

> the point of the book is ethical. . . . I wanted to write that my work consists of two parts: of the one which is here, and of everything I have *not* written. And precisely this second part is the important one. For the Ethical is delimited from within, as it were by my book; and I'm convinced that, *strictly speaking*, it can ONLY be delimited in this way. In brief, I think: All of that which *many* are *babbling* I have defined in my book by remaining silent about it.[8]

To be sure, Wittgenstein is exaggerating here the ethical aspect of the book, given that its main focus is actually logic and meta-physics, not ethics. After all, from the six years he spent writing this book, only a few months were dedicated to ethical questions. Maybe his exaggeration was due to the fact that his addressee was not a philosopher, but a literary publicist, indeed one whom Wittgenstein was trying to persuade to publish his book. One could even argue that the ethical ending of the book is parasitic on the main part dealing with logic, since he develops the distinction between saying and showing in the main part and then makes use of it in the passages on ethics. And indeed, when he wrote in the same year to a very different addressee, namely Russell, he emphasized that the main point of the book

> is the theory of what can be expressed by propositions – i.e. by language – (and, which comes to the same, what can be *thought*) and what cannot be expressed by propositions, but only shown (*gezeigt*); which, I believe, is the cardinal problem of philosophy.[9]

In conclusion, we could understand the logical part very well without the ethical one, but not vice versa. Wittgenstein's work had indeed extended from the foundations of logic to the nature of the world, and further to mysticism, but only in this order.

5

The Wilderness Years, 1918–29

The *Tractatus* was a highly original book, both in content and in form, and the author knew this. As soon as he finished the type-script in summer 1918, Wittgenstein submitted it to Jahoda and Siegel, the Viennese publishers of Kraus's journal *Die Fackel*, but it was rejected. A series of disappointing negotiations with several publishers ensued, including Braumüller in Vienna, who had pub-lished Weininger; Insel Verlag, the German publisher of Rilke, and von Ficker's journal *Der Brenner*. He even contacted a now forgotten philosophy journal, but when asked to transform the text into a more conventional format, Wittgenstein withdrew his offer. In these negotiations he received support from people like Russell, Frege, Rilke, but it was all to no avail. The value of the book escaped publishers and they thought it was too risky to publish a totally unknown author. One offer, for instance, by Braumüller, made the publication of the *Tractatus* conditional on Wittgenstein agreeing to cover the costs of paper and printing. Wittgenstein refused, saying

> I think it's not decent behaviour, from a social point of view,
> to force a book onto the world (of which the publisher is a part)
> in this way. *My* job was to write the book: its acceptance by the
> world must proceed in a normal fashion.[1]

The great difficulties he encountered in this affair left him most embittered. 'I don't know where I can get my work accepted either.

If I were only somewhere else than in this shitty world!' he wrote to von Ficker. The content of the book appeared not only to be unsayable, but even unprintable. By 1920, after yet another rejection, he had become so disillusioned that he wrote to Russell saying that he was giving up, leaving the manuscript to Russell to do with as he pleased. Russell commissioned one of his former pupils, the mathematician Dorothy Wrinch, to see to the publication of the book. After one last rejection, this time by Cambridge University Press, she approached several German journals and received a particularly positive reply from *Annalen der Naturphilosophie*, a journal now largely remembered because the *Tractatus* appeared there for the first time. As the journal's editor made clear to Wrinch, the typescript was accepted only because it was accompanied by a lengthy and sympathetic introduction by Russell, a celebrity by any estimate. The *Tractatus* was thus finally published in the first half of 1921, three years after its completion. Ironically, the *Annalen* stopped its publication with the *Tractatus*, as if to prove the point of the book's last proposition. Wittgenstein, who was not sent the proofs, disapproved of this first edition, calling it a pirated version because of the many printing mistakes concerning the logical notation. The *Tractatus* came out in a form acceptable to him only in 1922, this time published by Routledge and Kegan Paul, with an English translation accompanying the German original. The translation, reviewed and improved by Wittgenstein, was made by C. K. Ogden, a linguist, with assistance by Frank Ramsey, one of the most promising British philosophers of his generation.

For all its frustrating aspects, the publishing affair was only the first of many difficulties Wittgenstein would encounter in his post-war life. At the end of the war we find him in an Italian prisoner-of-war camp near Como. He remained in captivity for another eight months and was transferred to a camp in Cassino in January 1919. Naturally, circumstances in these camps were very different from those in the trenches. There was much idle time to kill, for instance through concerts, lectures, discussions, even exhibitions that the captives would organize. Wittgenstein participated in this camp life and established friendships with the sculptor Michael Drobil, the writer Franz Parak and the teacher Ludwig Hänsel. With the latter Wittgenstein discussed logic and read Kant's *Critique of Pure Reason*. They were to remain lifelong friends. Parak has provided us with the following description of Wittgenstein in the camp:

> He had a thin face and a noble profile, was of middle height . . . the really striking thing about him was his manner of speaking: it conveyed an extraordinary definiteness. There was a characteristic movement of his head too: usually it was bowed, but from time to time he would throw it back and direct his gaze into the distance.[2]

Reminding him of his time in Olmütz, these acquaintances provided Wittgenstein with some relief after the strain of the war. But they did not relieve him of his inner tensions and conflicts, which were no longer overshadowed by the much greater dangers of warfare. Indeed, if anything, under the burden of his recent experiences he had become even less capable of leading a normal life. Not unlike many of his generation who had witnessed the catastrophe of the 'Great War', only more intensely so, adaptation to civilian life was painful for him. The years in the army had fundamentally changed him. They had triggered a religious awakening and the desire to live a Tolstoyan life devoted to simple people. His lifestyle was now frugal and it would stay so for the rest of his life. He dressed in the simplest way possible, often wearing his old uniform, rejecting altogether the role of the wealthy young man before the war. He could not see any purpose for himself in the high society he originated from. Since he believed himself to have solved the problems of philosophy, the mediocrity of an academic career did not appeal to him. On his return from captivity, in August 1919, he decided to dispose of the fortune inherited from his father and did so immediately by distributing it among his sisters and brother, much to the dismay of his financial adviser, who considered this simply an act of suicide. According to Parak he briefly contemplated becoming a priest.[3] But the compromises of institutionalized religion were still unacceptable to him. Thus he settled for becoming a primary school teacher, because as a teacher he could 'read the gospel with the children'.[4] His family was not pleased with this decision and felt that Ludwig was wasting his talent on a mediocre profession – we can imagine how much less pleased his father Karl would have been, had he been alive. As Hermine put it: it was as if one used a precision tool to open a packing case! But Wittgenstein felt that he was not understood, as a striking simile in a reply to Hermine indicates: 'You remind me of someone looking through a window who can't make sense of the strange movements of a passer-by outside. He has no idea of the violence of the storm outside nor of the difficulty the other has simply in staying on his feet.'[5]

So in September 1919 he enrolled in a teacher's training college in Vienna, and at the end of the course in July 1920 the man whom Russell had expected before the war to make the next big step in philosophy was a certified primary school teacher. The course itself was easy. Given his educational background, he was respected by the college faculty and was spared most academic subjects. But the experience of sitting in a schoolroom again was actually very humiliating. 'The benches are full of boys of 17 and 18 and I've reached 30. That leads to some very funny situations – and many *very* unpleasant ones too! I often feel miserable.'[6] As in Linz or on the *Goplana* he felt once again ostracized, although this time his misery was self-inflicted.

The period was generally one of great depression, causing him to contemplate suicide once more. He felt not at ease with himself, being in a 'terrible state of mind' and having 'no faith', as he described it in letters to Paul Engelmann:

> I feel like completely emptying myself again; I have had a most miserable time lately. Of course only as a result of my own baseness and rottenness. I have continually thought of taking my own life, and the idea still haunts me sometimes. *I have sunk to the lowest point.* May you never experience this.[7]

Exactly why he thought so little of himself is not clear, even if we take into account the humiliation in the college and the trouble of finding a publisher for the *Tractatus*.[8] There were also the pressures from his family, whom he tried to keep at arm's length by moving out of the aristocratic lodgings and into a flat, and, more importantly, the feeling that his philosophical work was not understood by anybody. He had sent copies of the book to Frege and Russell, the two most able contemporary philosophers in his eyes. Frege sent him some comments and questions of clarification concerning the opening pages of the *Tractatus*. Wittgenstein was very disappointed by these, as he felt Frege had no understanding of the deep issues in the book. For similar reasons he was not happy with Russell's feedback either. Russell, who was very enthusiastic about the book, agreed to meet Wittgenstein in The Hague during the Christmas vacation of 1919 to have Wittgenstein explain the book to him. Since Wittgenstein was now without money and in need of funding for the trip, he asked Russell to sell the belongings he had left in Cambridge, including the expensive furniture he had bought in 1913, a deal that was carried out to the financial advantage of Russell. Wittgenstein also asked Russell to burn all his Cambridge diaries and manuscripts. Soon after the meeting Russell wrote his introduction to the *Tractatus*, but Wittgenstein was so disappointed by his former teacher's apparent lack of understanding that he initially decided against publishing the book at all rather than have

The veteran: Wittgenstein in the early post-war years.

it appear with such a preface. Fortunately, Russell took this rejection lightly and resumed his efforts to find a publisher for the *Tractatus*, with eventual success as discussed above.

Tormented by his inner demons, Wittgenstein finally fled the metropolis and spent the summer of 1920 working as a gardener in the Klosterneuburg monastery outside Vienna. To describe this refuge as therapy would go too far, but it certainly had relaxing effects on his battered soul. The gardening work was purely manual and simple, but exhausting enough to distract him from plunging into the ever-threatening inner abyss. One particular reason for his overall depressive state can be gathered from a letter to Russell he wrote from here: 'Every day I think of Pinsent. He took half my life away with him. The devil will take the other half.'[9]

In September 1920 Wittgenstein was offered a position as a teacher in a prosperous town near Vienna, which he rejected because it had 'a park with a fountain' and was thus not rural enough for his taste. Instead, he settled for Trattenbach in the mountains of Lower Austria, a poor and remote village. One might think that he now had a chance to realize his Tolstoyan ideal and thus actually become happy. But his six years as a schoolteacher in Austria (1920–26) were overall of little joy and self-realization. This was in part due to Tolstoy's ill-conceived romantic ideal of serving the so-called simple people, an ideal that has exerted a seductive power on many modern intellectuals. Wittgenstein was not immune to it. In addition, his friend Hänsel encouraged him to join the Reform School Movement that was taking shape within a wider social reform in post-war Austria. Although Wittgenstein was not an explicit advocate of this movement (in contrast to, say, the philosopher and later opponent Karl Popper, who was also a schoolteacher in Austria during the same period), he was not opposed to the movement's focus on new techniques of teaching, in particular the focus on learning by doing instead of learning by drilling. Wittgenstein intended to 'better' simple people by teaching them mathematics, the German classics and the Bible, probably a far too idealistic project, ignoring the real-life concerns of rural people. Additional handicaps that doomed the experiment from the outset were Wittgenstein's irascible character and his wealthy origin. He was soon revolted by the peasant society in which he found himself, and the dislike was reciprocated.

Initially, however, Wittgenstein was rather pleased with his new home, describing it as beautiful and tiny. To Russell, who was guest lecturing through China at the time, he wrote: 'It must be the first time that the schoolmaster at Trattenbach has ever corresponded with a professor in Peking.'[10] Friends like Hänsel, Drobil and Sjögren visited him at weekends, contributing to his improving mood. He also befriended the local priest, Alois Neururer, to whom he read aloud Dostoevsky's *The Brothers Karamazov*. As for his pupils, he managed to fascinate them, at least initially. His teaching methods were unconventional. Instead of forcing them to learn something by heart, he tried to raise their interest about a problem and motivate them to find out the correct solution by themselves. The greatest successes were achieved when he could take advantage of his various skills, teaching them how to build a steam engine or a tower, draw human figures in motion, assemble a cat's skeleton, identify the architectural style of buildings during a trip to Vienna, etc. His sister Hermine witnessed her brother in action:

> The interest that he aroused was enormous. Even the ungifted and usually inattentive among the boys came up with astonishingly good answers, and they were positively climbing over each other in their eagerness to be given a chance to answer or to demonstrate a point.[11]

In one case, his engineering skills even helped him earn some recognition from the villagers. This was when, after failed attempts by several engineers, Wittgenstein managed to repair the engine in the local textile factory simply by directing four workers each to hit a particular spot with a hammer in the order dictated by and comprehensible only to him. This incident became something of a legend in Trattenbach and was referred to as a 'miracle'.

Unfortunately, however, such successes did not suffice to gain the trust of the villagers. He was viewed as an awkward stranger, a 'rich baron' visited by wealthy people from Vienna. They found his decision to live in their community baffling. Their opinion worsened when Wittgenstein began to show weaknesses in his teaching. He demanded high standards from his pupils and was willing to give them time and attention without stint if they seemed promising. With the best pupils, who revered him, he even arranged extra tuition. But he showed much less patience with weak students. Since he was irascible and believed in the effectiveness of corporal punishment, contrary to the doctrines of the Reform Movement, he often hit his pupils for misbehaviour, but often also for what seemed to him to be stupidity. This was especially the case if they were girls and failed in his beloved subject, mathematics, taught not only for two hours every morning, but also at a level higher than required by the curriculum.[12] He was soon feared by his pupils, disliked by their parents and disapproved of by his colleagues. Here is a vivid recollection by one of his victims:

> During the arithmetic lesson we that had algebra had to sit in the first row. My friend Anna Völkerer and I one day decided not to give any answers. Wittgenstein asked: 'What do you have?' To the question what is three times six Anna said: 'I don't know.' He asked me how many metres are there in a kilometre. I said nothing and received a box on my ears. Later Wittgenstein said: 'If you don't know I will take a child from the youngest class in the school who will know.' After the lesson Wittgenstein took me into the office and asked: 'Is it that you don't want to or is it that you can't?' I said 'Yes, I want to.' Wittgenstein said to me: 'You are a good student, but as for arithmetic . . . Or are you ill? Do you have a headache?' Then I lied, 'Yes!' 'Then', said Wittgenstein, 'please, please Brenner, can you forgive me?' While he said this he held up his hands in prayer. I immediately felt my lie to be a great disgrace.[13]

The schoolteacher and his pupils: Wittgenstein and schoolchildren in Puchberg am Schneeberg, Austria.

There were similar incidents. Wittgenstein sometimes regretted his outbursts and at least in one case he went to the house of a pupil to ask for her forgiveness. But one cannot really feel sorry for Wittgenstein in this context. He was inflicting futile pain on children for not mastering his venerated discipline, of little use to them in their social context. His rueful reflections on his failures did not lead to the only acceptable conclusion: to *change* his teaching methods, indeed his whole attitude to teaching at a primary school. Instead, he was inclined to view the lack of success in his new profession as a sign of the primitiveness of the villagers and, no less important, his longstanding moral flaws. Thus, in early 1921 he wrote to Engelmann:

> I have been morally dead for more than a year! . . . I am one of those cases which perhaps are not all that rare today: I had a task, did not do it, and now the failure is wrecking my life. I ought to have done something positive with my life, to have become a star in the sky. Instead of which I remained stuck on earth, and now I am gradually fading out. My life has really

become meaningless and so it consists only of futile episodes. The people around me do not notice this and would not understand; but I know that I have a fundamental deficiency.[14]

The summer vacation of 1921 Wittgenstein spent in Norway with Arvid Sjögren, finally seeing again the house he had built in 1913. His companion's family were close friends of the Wittgensteins. Ludwig had made friends with Arvid while he had lodged with the Sjögrens in Vienna during his teaching course. Arvid, the future husband of Ludwig's niece Clara, was a big and gruff young man who regarded Wittgenstein as his mentor and who followed the latter's advice to become a mechanic instead of going to university. Wittgenstein gave similar, not unproblematic, advice several times later. Arvid was, as Monk suggests, Wittgenstein's first disciple, with many more to come.[15]

The following school year Wittgenstein was back in Trattenbach, but due to his growing difficulties he was transferred a year later, in September 1922, to a secondary school in another village, Hassbach. However, he disliked the new environment as well, finding the pretentiousness of his colleagues, whom he described as being 'not human *at all* but loathsome worms', unbearable. In November he transferred to a different village, Puchberg, which was also in the mountains. Although his current life was far removed from philosophy, in this year he spent considerable time revising the English translation of the *Tractatus*.

The year 1922 also saw the final break-up of the friendship with Russell. They had decided to meet in Innsbruck in August and due to the many tourists profiting from the inflation in Austria they were forced to share a hotel room. Russell's wife Dora, who was accompanying her husband, witnessed no open quarrel, but the differences were deep. While Russell was now in favour of socialism, a staunch atheist and libertarian about sex, Wittgenstein was at the height of his religious ardour, leading a chaste and apolitical life. Russell, who had by now given up theoretical philosophy and was, through popular lectures and writings on politics and ethics, in the course of becoming the famous public intellectual as which he is still known, was partly amused, partly repelled by Wittgenstein's attempts to convince him 'with great earnestness that it is better to be good than clever'.[16] Wittgenstein, on the other hand, must have been repelled by what he considered to be a frivolous lifestyle on the part of Russell. Shocked by the disaster of the war, Russell believed in the urgency of changing the world, while Wittgenstein was more introverted, seeking primarily to change himself. When Heinrich Postl, a local coalminer from Puchberg, expressed his wish to improve the world, Wittgenstein replied: 'Just improve yourself; that is the only thing you *can* do to better the world.' In short, crucial things separated Russell and Wittgenstein. Whether it was Wittgenstein or Russell who broke off the contact is not entirely clear, although the evidence suggests it was Russell, since he did not reply to Wittgenstein's subsequent letters. In any case, the clash produced by these different ethical outlooks was definitive: they were never again to address each other as friends, but only as colleagues. Years later Wittgenstein is reported to have said apropos of Russell's ethical writings, in particular those on marriage and free love:

> If a person tells me he has been at the worst places I have no right to judge him; but if he tells me it was his superior wisdom that enabled him to go there, then I know he is a fraud. . . . Russell's books should be bound in two colours, those dealing with mathematical logic in red – and all students of philosophy should read them; those dealing with ethics and politics in blue – and no one should be allowed to read them.[17]

Wittgenstein spent two years in the village of Puchberg and they were similar to those in Trattenbach, save for his friendship with

Postl and Rudolf Koder, a gifted pianist with whom he could play music, preferably Brahms. One other welcome digression was the visit of his English translator Frank Ramsey in September 1923. There could hardly have been a more suited discussion partner for Wittgenstein. Ramsey was the most able young philosopher in Cambridge and author of an insightful, if critical, review of the *Tractatus*. He stayed for two weeks in Puchberg, during which they spent several hours every day reading and discussing the *Tractatus*. Wittgenstein even made some corrections to both the English and the German versions of his book following these discussions. Ramsey much admired Wittgenstein. He wrote in 1924 to his mother: 'We really live in a great time for thinking, with Einstein, Freud and Wittgenstein all alive, and all in Germany or Austria, those foes of civilisation!' From Ramsey's point of view Wittgenstein's schoolteacher career was, as he wrote to Keynes, a 'ridiculous waste of his energy and brain'. Together with Keynes Ramsey tried to convince Wittgenstein to come back to Cambridge and continue philosophy. Keynes offered to fund his trip, while Ramsey enquired about Wittgenstein's formal requirements for obtaining a PhD. But it was to no avail.

> He says he himself will do nothing more, not because he is bored, but because his mind is no longer flexible. He says no one can do more than 5 or 10 years work at philosophy. (His book took 7.) And he is sure that Russell will do nothing more important. . . . He is very poor . . . He has one *tiny* room whitewashed, containing a bed, washstand, small table and one hard chair and that is all there is room for. His evening meal, which I shared last night, is rather unpleasant coarse bread, butter and cocoa.[18]

The contrast between this lifestyle and that of the rest of Wittgenstein's family, whom Ramsey visited a few months later, could not have been greater. In Vienna Ramsey witnessed the

Wittgenstein's philosopher friend Frank Ramsey, who died at a tragically young age.

incredible wealth of Wittgenstein's family, for instance when he attended a party organized by Ludwig's sister Margarete in her lodgings, the Schönborn Palace. Ramsey also witnessed the worries of the family, who desired so much to get the prodigal son out of the wilderness, a desire that was frustrated by the fact that he rejected any kind of help they were offering. Having some interest in psychoanalysis, Ramsey ventured an explanation for Wittgenstein's state of mind: the 'terribly strict upbringing. Three of his brothers committed suicide – they were made to work so hard by their father: at one time the eight children had twenty-six private tutors; and their mother took no interest in them.'

Although Wittgenstein refused to return to Cambridge, Ramsey's visit refreshed his connections with England, which eventually led him to visit some of his English friends in 1925. Meanwhile, his life in the wilderness continued. In September 1924 he transferred to the primary school in Otterthal, a village close to Trattenbach and equally poor. These villages, and the town of Kirchberg, the district's capital, have now become almost pilgrimage locations. Philosophical symposia, attended by Wittgenstein experts from all over the world, take place every summer in Kirchberg. One can trace Wittgenstein's steps by following designated paths which are marked by quotes from the *Tractatus* at intervals. And with some luck one can still meet a village elder who can remember Wittgenstein. In any case, it was here that Wittgenstein's teaching career ended in an ungraceful manner in April 1926. Once again he was not in control of himself in class and hit a boy on the head several times. The boy, who was of weak health, collapsed. Wittgenstein called in panic for a doctor and then left the school in a hurry. There was a public hearing of the case, apparently at his own request, but Wittgenstein was acquitted, partly because he lied about the extent to which he had applied corporal punishment in his classes.[19] Humiliated and morally defeated, he decided to give up teaching for good.

There has been some speculation that despite its sorry ending, Wittgenstein's career as a schoolteacher was of great significance for his philosophical development. Indeed, it is claimed that his time as a teacher is visible on almost every page of his *Philosophical Investigations*.[20] However, although there are several passages discussing infant language acquisition in his later book, this claim is widely exaggerated. Nevertheless, there remains the possibility that the teaching experience shifted his focus away from the abstract, mathematical approach to language of Frege and Russell toward the more down-to-earth and applied aspects of language as they characteristically arise in the teaching of children. Paul Engelmann has suggested that the experience of teaching is reflected in the less sibylline and more unassuming style of Wittgenstein's later writings.

When this man, who until then – for all the depth of his insight into the essence of life and humanity – had been frighteningly unworldly and hopelessly foreign to human society, was suddenly brought face to face with its grisly reality, he was luckily also brought into direct contact with children.[21]

Be this as it may, there is one more palpable result of his teaching experience. Wishing to improve his pupils' spelling, Wittgenstein considered introducing dictionaries in his classes, but realized that the ones available on the market were too expensive. Thus he set out to write a short and affordable spelling dictionary for primary schools, partly based on spelling lists he compiled with his pupils. The dictionary, which was tailored to the needs of primary schools and even reflected some peculiarities of the local dialect, proved very effective and quickly improved the children's spelling. It was the second, and last, book Wittgenstein would publish in his life-time.[22] The 40-page dictionary appeared in 1926 and had a notable circulation, but was not a commercial success and therefore was not reprinted. Nevertheless, it was a remarkable attempt by Wittgenstein and proof of how seriously he approached any field of activity. It is almost comical that he has been portrayed recently as a dyslexic and that aspects of his philosophical work have been attributed to this alleged disability.[23] A dyslexic who wrote a spelling dictionary?

His lack of success as a teacher greatly depressed Wittgenstein and gave him, once again, the feeling that there was no *Sitz im Leben*, no place for him in this world. He contemplated again the possibility of becoming a monk, but was told that this was not the right motive for joining monastic life. Instead he started working as a gardener for the monks in Hütteldorf outside Vienna, living there for three months in almost hermitic conditions in a shed in the gar-den of the monastery. Despite appearances, this episode marked the beginning of his gradual return to society. In June 1926 his mother died in Vienna. This event seems to have overcome his estrange-ment with the family, which dated back to at least 1913, when his father died.[24] Wittgenstein began now to participate enthusiastically in family life. Moreover, he was given the ideal opportunity to inte-grate fully with society when his sister Margarete commissioned Paul Engelmann to design and build a mansion for her in the

Kundmanngasse in Vienna. Spurred on by an interest in architecture and the artistic ideals he shared with Engelmann, Wittgenstein accepted an invitation to join the project. Although Engelmann had already largely designed the plan of the building, Wittgenstein soon dominated the actual building process, making several changes to the building, especially the interiors.

This new task, which occupied him until the end of 1928, was taken very seriously by Wittgenstein. Indeed, he saw it as his new vocation. Despite having no diploma, he was listed in the city directory as a professional architect, and his letters bore the letterhead 'Paul Engelmann & Ludwig Wittgenstein Architects'. Under Wittgenstein's careful eye, the doors and door handles were all made entirely of metal and designed according to strict mathematical relations referring to the dimensions of the rooms. The design also reflected Wittgenstein's hermitic lifestyle: bulbs were supposed to hang naked from the ceiling, and small, L-shaped radiators, which took a year to produce and were placed discreetly in the corners, remained unpainted. Every piece was uniquely crafted, in stark contrast to modern mass production.[25] There were also technical innovations, such as 150-kilogram metal screens that replaced curtains and could be lowered effortlessly to the floor. Wittgenstein's attention to detail was so fanatical that just when everybody thought the building was finished, he ordered the workers to raise the ceiling of one of the big rooms by 30 millimetres to satisfy his desired proportions. He was asked by a worker: 'Tell me, Herr Ingenieur, does a millimetre here or there really matter so much to you?' To which Herr Ingenieur thundered 'Yes!'[26] Needless to say there were other occasions on which he drove the builders to despair.

Being of plain shape and having no external decoration, it may seem obvious to say that the house strictly followed, indeed radicalized, Loos's rejection of any ornament. It has also been compared to buildings in the Bauhaus style. However, recent interpretations have

The house Wittgenstein designed for his sister Margarete in Kundmangasse, Vienna.

denied that the house is Loosian or Bauhausian.[27] It was not built according to the principles of Bauhaus functionalism, and the Wittgensteins, including Ludwig, had distanced themselves from Loos by the 1920s. Instead, it must be seen as a unique statement made by Wittgenstein, embodying absolute precision as a design principle and thus the spirit of the *Tractatus*. Hermine Wittgenstein, who admired its perfection and monumentality, could not see herself living in it, describing it as 'house embodied logic' and 'a dwelling for the gods'. Wittgenstein himself saw this lack of life as a specific deficiency, as he wrote later about his house:

> Within all great art there is a WILD animal: tamed. Not, e.g., in Mendelssohn. All great art has primitive human drives as its ground bass. They are not the *melody* (as they are, perhaps, in Wagner), but they are what gives the melody *depth & power*. In *this* sense one may call Mendelssohn a '*reproductive*' artist. – In the same sense: my house for Gretl is the product of a decidedly

sensitive ear, *good* manners, the expression of great *understanding* (for a culture, etc.). But *primordial* life, *wild* life striving to erupt into the open – is lacking. And so you might say, *health* is lacking (Kierkegaard). (Hothouse plant.)[28]

Some interpreters have claimed that the building exemplifies certain doctrines of the *Tractatus*, such as the showing–saying distinction. For, as we can read in a contemporary guide, in building this house Wittgenstein 'drew a clear demarcation between the effable and the ineffable as well, namely by stripping the syntax of classical architecture of all rhetoric and bringing it back to the point of origin where one can see it "sub specie aeternitatis"'.[29]

There is, however, a danger of exaggerating Wittgenstein's contribution to the house. First, too much is made of the parallel with his philosophy. Wittgenstein himself never claimed such a parallel. The formal-aesthetic similarities between his philosophical writings and his architectural project share a common source, namely certain aesthetic preferences, but nothing else. It is false to explain the *Tractatus* saying–showing distinction in terms of 'stripping the syntax of all rhetoric'. While the *style* of the *Tractatus* may indeed be seen as stripped of rhetoric, the *theory* of syntax has nothing to do with rhetoric. It is a complex philosophical doctrine and, whether true or not, could be expressed in other ways. Second, Wittgenstein's cultural models should not be underestimated. His later personal disapproval of Loos does not nullify the latter's influence. The influence of Weininger and Kraus lies in the background as well. Third, Engelmann's contribution, namely the ground plan, should not be ignored. Although Engelmann later wrote that he considered Wittgenstein the chief architect, this overly modest claim is likely to have reflected his deep admiration for Wittgenstein. Finally, we have Margarete's voice, which had much weight and which, given her latent traditionalism, counterbalanced Ludwig's austerity. This traditionalism revealed itself in her choice to have her mansion imitate the room distribution of the Palais Wittgenstein, to have an entry hall and haute-bourgeois furnishings, such as carpets, curtains, Rococo chairs, statues, Chinese vases and plants.[30] It is telling that despite this *Stilbruch* there was no disagreement between the siblings. Two years before his death, Wittgenstein wrote to his sister, 'Yesterday I thought . . . of the Kundmanngasse house and how delightfully you furnished it and how comforting. In these matters we understand each other.'[31]

After the Second World War the house went through a troubled history, including its partial devastation by Soviet soldiers, who used it as barracks in 1945. In the 1970s it was saved in the last moment from demolition and declared a national monument. In 1975 Communist Bulgaria bought it and turned it into a cultural centre. It can be visited today, although little of the original interior remains. Ironically, it stands not far away from the more famous Hundertwasser House, which, with its biomorphic and colourful design, could not be more diametrically opposed to Wittgenstein's architecture. Hundertwasser rejected even the idea of a straight line, calling it 'the devil's tool'. One wonders how an encounter between Wittgenstein and Hundertwasser would have turned out.

Not long after completing the house, Wittgenstein's and Engelmann's friendship deteriorated. The reasons for this are a matter of speculation, but one plausible explanation is that in 1928 Wittgenstein was introduced to a wealthy young Swiss woman and art student, Marguerite Respinger, who had an aversion to Engelmann. Respinger was a friend of the family and Wittgenstein courted her for around three years – his only heterosexual relationship that we know of. The nature of the relationship was peculiar, given their remarkable differences. Marguerite was almost half Ludwig's age and had no interest in philosophy and spiritual matters, but rather in an entertaining lifestyle. Their only common interest was art. Nevertheless, encouraged by Margarete, who saw in Marguerite's indifferent attitude to intellectual matters precisely the distraction needed for her brother's tortured mind, they began dating, meeting almost daily for the cinema or in some Viennese café. Wittgenstein even sculpted a bust inspired by her in the studio of his friend Michael Drobil, in whose work he took a critical interest. Wittgenstein has sometimes been portrayed as a homosexual, but judging from his relationship with Marguerite this may be not entirely accurate. Not only did they kiss, but his diaries from this period show that Ludwig was clearly in love with Marguerite, taking the relationship very seriously, probably more so than she.

> I love Marguerite very much & am very anxious that she might not be healthy since I haven't gotten a letter from her in more than a week. When I am alone I think of her again & again but at other times too. Were I more decent, my love for her would be more decent too. And yet I love her now as tenderly as I can.[32]

> I am very much in love with R., have been for a long time of course, but it is especially strong now. And yet I know that the matter is in all probability hopeless. That is, I must be braced that she might get engaged & married any moment. And I know that this will be *very* painful for me. I therefore know that I should not hang my whole weight on this rope since I know that eventually it will give. That is I should remain standing with both feet on firm ground & only hold the rope but not hang on it. But that is difficult. It is difficult to love so unselfishly that one holds on to love & does not want to be held by it.[33]

Marriage was seriously considered, but both expected very different things from it. Ludwig envisaged marriage as a spiritual, maybe even celibate communion (not unlike Kafka with his Felice, although for very different reasons) and did not want to have children, since he considered it irresponsible to give life to a person

Two significant women in Wittgenstein's life: Marguerite Respinger and Margarete Stonborough, 1931.

in this world of misery. Marguerite certainly wanted children. When she visited him in Norway in 1931, his behaviour towards her brought out these differences in such a drastic manner that she decided he would be the last man on earth she would want to marry. To begin with, Ludwig arranged that they live in different houses. He spent little time with her, instead reading the Bible, praying and preparing mentally for the holy act of marriage. She on the other hand went swimming, took walks, socialized with the villagers, and ignored the copy of the Bible he had slipped into her luggage.[34] How could they ever have lived up to each other's expectations? After two weeks she left Norway disenchanted and that was the end of the relationship. But they stayed good friends. In 1933 Marguerite married one of the Sjögrens, a decision Wittgenstein was very unhappy with, but which he came to accept. Marguerite wrote later in her memoirs:

> Ludwig came to see me . . . an hour before my wedding. 'You are taking a boat, the sea will be rough, remain always attached to me so that you don't capsize', he said to me. Until that very moment I had not realized his deep attachment nor perhaps his great deception. For years I have been like soft putty in his hands which he had worked to shape into a better being. He had been like a Samaritan who gives new life to someone who is failing.[35]

As good as Wittgenstein's intentions might have been toward Respinger, her influence on him seems to have been more nefarious. We have no clear evidence of her anti-Semitism, but we do know that Respinger disliked Engelmann because he was 'the sort of Jew one didn't like'.[36] It was during his time with her that Wittgenstein, at least temporarily, revised his views on his Jewishness and Jews in general, and we find remarks about this topic in his diary around 1931. As Ray Monk has pointed out, if they had not been written by Wittgenstein, we could understand these remarks as the rantings of an anti-Semite.[37] Jews are described as having a 'secretive and cunning nature' that is independent of their long persecution. Wittgenstein comments on the traditional anti-Semitic comparison of Jews with a tumour in the body of European civilization without any disapproval, and he describes the Jews as merely reproductive, unable genuinely to create anything, 'even the tiniest flower or blade of grass'. Finally, he applies this cliché to himself, writing (note, incidentally, the interesting list of influences):

> The saint is the only Jewish 'genius'. Even the greatest Jewish thinker is no more than talented. (Myself for instance.) I think there is some truth in my idea that I am really only reproductive in my thinking. I think I have never *invented* a line of thinking but that it was always provided for me by someone else & I have done no more than passionately take it up for my work of clarification. That is how Boltzmann, Hertz, Schopenhauer, Frege, Russell, Kraus, Loos, Weininger Spengler, Sraffa have influenced me . . . It is typical of the Jewish mind to understand someone's else work better than he understands it himself.[38]

Not all his diary notes on Jews display this negative attitude. For instance, Wittgenstein also writes: 'The Jew is a desert region, but underneath its thin layer of rock lies the molten lava of spirit and intellect.'[39] Nevertheless, what surprises one about all these passages is his readiness to make sweeping remarks about 'the Jew'. It contrasts sharply with the much more critical attitude towards this kind of talk that he himself displayed in later years. Norman Malcolm reports that when in 1939 he remarked to Wittgenstein that the British national character was incompatible with plotting a bomb against Hitler (as rumour had it at the time), Wittgenstein was so outraged that he stopped seeing his friend for a while. Even after five years he remained shocked by the primitiveness of Malcolm's remark:

> what is the use of studying philosophy if all that it does for you is to enable you to talk with some plausibility about some abstruse questions of logic, etc., & if it does not improve your thinking about the important questions of everyday life, if it does not make you more conscientious than any . . . journalist.[40]

This critique could also have been levied against Wittgenstein's 1931 remarks on Jews. One possible explanation for those remarks, advanced by Monk, is that throughout his life Wittgenstein constantly questioned and doubted himself, from both a philosophical and a moral point of view, and that during that brief period under Respinger's spell he voiced his doubts in the language of anti-Semitism.[41] This is a plausible, if charitable interpretation of a man who placed the independence of his judgements above everything else. Note that even after 1931 Wittgenstein held an ambiguous attitude to his Jewish origins – despite a cryptic remark to Maurice Drury in 1949 that his thoughts are 'one hundred percent Hebraic'. Thus in his 1936 confession, presented to close friends and family members, he admitted that he had let many people believe he was only one-quarter Jewish. This proves not only that Wittgenstein felt Jewish, but that he perceived Jewishness as a matter of shame and concealment. After all, he had grown up in a virulently anti-Semitic city, Karl Lueger's Vienna, and it is implausible to assume that this had no effect on his self-perception. To give just one example, when young Ludwig wanted to join a gym in Vienna, which was open only to 'Aryans', he was determined to lie about his Jewish background in order to obtain membership until dissuaded by his brother Paul.[42] A good way of concluding the matter was offered by David Stern:

> There is no doubt that Wittgenstein was of Jewish descent; it is equally clear that he was not a practicing Jew. But insofar as he thought of himself as Jewish, he did so in terms of the anti-Semitic prejudices of his time. It would have been good if he could have untangled those prejudices, but he did not do so.[43]

6

Return to Cambridge and Philosophy, 1929–39

Wittgenstein's 'wilderness' years were not dedicated to philosophy, although he maintained contacts with Russell and Ramsey. Since he believed that he had solved all the problems of philosophy, what he looked for after the completion of the *Tractatus* was a place in life. With this he was only to a small degree successful. Wittgenstein was born for philosophy and his renunciation of philosophy could not be permanent. Other problems became temporally more important, but philosophy always resurfaced as a necessity. 'Art alone . . . had not been enough for him on which to build a proper life. But it was an indispensable part of the foundation of it.'[1] Max Brod's words about Kafka could fit Wittgenstein just as well, if we replace 'art' with 'philosophy'. Unlike Rimbaud, for instance, who completed his entire poetical *oeuvre* as a young man and then settled for a different, more conventional life without literary ambitions, Wittgenstein's relation to philosophy is more comparable to a comet, which is initially attracted by the sun, approaches it, begins to glow, is then hurled away, and finally returns again, this time glowing even more intensely.

During the years of his hermitic retreat the 'egg' that he had laid with the *Tractatus* began to attract more and more attention, both in Austria and abroad. Ramsey's visit in 1923 was a consequence of the immense interest the book sparked in Cambridge. Philosophers closer to home were also keen to meet the author of the enigmatic book. One such philosopher was Moritz Schlick, who from 1924 onwards headed a group of academics, mostly philosophers, but also mathematicians, logicians and physicists, later known as the Vienna Circle. Some of their most prominent members were Rudolf Carnap, Otto Neurath, Hans Reichenbach, Herbert Feigl, Kurt Gödel and Friedrich Waismann. After the Nazis came to power, some of them emigrated to the USA and had a major impact on the rise of analytic philosophy there. What united them from the outset was a strictly scientific world-view. They venerated natural science, epitomized by modern physics, as the only way to gain knowledge about the world and achieve social progress, and they rejected religion and the metaphysical systems of traditional philosophy as unscientific and irrational. As logical empiricists (or logical positivists) they believed that all knowledge can be reduced to sensory experience and can be given a precise formulation by means of logical analysis. They hugely admired the *Tractatus* because in their view it had formulated the programme for a strictly scientific method in philosophy for the first time. In their manifesto of 1929, *The Scientific Conception of the World: The Vienna Circle*, they hailed Einstein, Russell and Wittgenstein as the main representatives of the scientific world-view. It seems that the members of the Vienna Circle did not fully realize, or chose to ignore, that the author of the *Tractatus* did not share their world-view at all. He too believed that the statements of traditional metaphysics were nonsensical, but not because there were no metaphysical truths, rather because such truths were ineffable. His view was: everything that can be said, can be said clearly, and we must pass over the rest in silence. Their view was: everything that can be said, can be said clearly, and there is nothing else. Moreover, Wittgenstein did not share their belief in social progress by means of science. In fact his view in this matter was diametrically opposed to the Vienna Circle and more akin to the pessimism of Oswald Spengler's *The Decline of the West*, a book he read avidly in 1930. It was in this year that he wrote a lengthy preface for a planned book, *Philosophical Remarks*, in which he stated:

This book is written for those who are in sympathy with the spirit in which it is written. This spirit is, I believe, different from that of the prevailing European and American civilization. The spirit of *this civilization* the expression of which is the industry, architecture, music, of present day fascism & socialism, is a *spirit that is alien & uncongenial* to the author. . . . Even if it is clear to me then that the disappearance of a culture does not signify the disappearance of human value but simply of certain means of expressing this value, still the fact remains that I contemplate the current of European civilization without sympathy, without understanding its aims if any. So I am really writing for friends who are scattered throughout the corners of the globe. It is all one to me whether the typical western scientist understands or appreciates my work since in any case he does not understand the spirit in which I write. Our civilization is characterized by the word 'progress'. Progress is its form, it is not one of its properties that it makes progress. *Typically* it constructs. Its *activity* is to construct a more and more complicated structure. And even clarity is only a means to this end & not an end in itself. – For me on the contrary clarity, transparency, is an end in itself – I am not interested in erecting a building but in having the foundations of possible buildings transparently before me. – So I am aiming at something different than are the scientists & my thoughts move differently than do theirs.[2]

Wittgenstein never gave up his distrust of progress. Towards the end of his life he wrote:

It isn't absurd . . . to believe that the age of science and technology is the beginning of the end for humanity; that the idea of great progress is a delusion, along with the idea that the truth will ultimately be known; that there is nothing good or desirable about scientific knowledge and that mankind, in seeking it, is falling into a trap. It is by no means obvious that this is not how things are.[3]

In his opposition to a scientific civilization Wittgenstein was joined by many other contemporary thinkers all over Europe, not only by the above-mentioned Weininger and Spengler, but also José Ortega y Gasset, Giovanni Gentile and Martin Heidegger. Heidegger, to mention the most illustrious example, wrote at the time:

> Russia and America, seen metaphysically, are both the same: the same hopeless frenzy of unchained technology and of the rootless organization of the average man . . . The spiritual decline of the earth has progressed so far that peoples are in danger of losing their last spiritual strength, the strength that makes it possible even to see the decline . . . the darkening of the world, the flight of the gods, the destruction of the earth, the reduction of human beings to a mass, the hatred and mistrust of everything creative and free.[4]

This distrust of modernity and science deeply separated Wittgenstein from the Vienna Circle. Nevertheless, the logical positivists saw in Wittgenstein their most important philosophical forerunner. Schlick spent two years reading the *Tractatus* line by line with his colleagues, and eventually resolved to meet the author himself. Their attempts to contact Wittgenstein in his villages in the mountains were initially unsuccessful and only in 1927, after Wittgenstein's return to Vienna, did they finally meet. Schlick persuaded him to meet them on a regular basis, although, given his sensitivity and frail state of mind, Schlick had to assure Wittgenstein that they would not ask him any direct questions, indeed that they would not even have to talk about philosophy. Ironically, these scientifically minded philosophers were so much under Wittgenstein's spell that sometimes their meetings had the character of a session between a guru and his disciples. He could talk and behave as he wanted – and he did. Sometimes he talked about religion, art and ethics. In one instance Wittgenstein turned his back to his audience and recited poems by Rabindranath Tagore, hardly an exponent of the scientific world-view! (Wittgenstein thought so highly of Tagore that later he translated a part of a play by the Indian poet for private use.) It was almost as if he was teaching them a lesson very different from that of positivistic philosophy.

With time, however, valuable philosophical discussions developed between them, some of which were recorded by Waismann and published as *Wittgenstein and the Vienna Circle* (1967). Most of these discussions focused on themes from the *Tractatus* such as the nature of language, logic, mathematics. But they also covered metaphysical themes, which the Vienna Circle members abhorred. Thus, he surprised his audience by expressing his sympathy with Schopenhauer, Kierkegaard and Heidegger. Heidegger, for instance, wrote in his *Being and Time* (1927): 'That in the face of which one has anxiety is Being-in-the-world as such . . . That in the face of which one has anxiety is not an entity within-the-world . . . the world as such is that in the face of which one has anxiety.'[5] Sentences like these are according to the *Tractatus* pure nonsense, and Rudolf Carnap, faithfully executing the programme of logical analysis, famously ridiculed Heidegger for such philosophical prose in an article in 1931. But Wittgenstein did not. For what Heidegger was trying to say could not be said, but it was, contrary to Carnap's belief, the most essential matter.

I can imagine what Heidegger means by Being and anxiety. Man feels the urge to run up against the limits of language. Think for example of the astonishment that anything at all exists. This astonishment cannot be expressed in the form of a question, and there is also no answer whatsoever. Anything we might say is *a priori* bound to be mere nonsense. Nevertheless we do run up against the limits of language. Kierkegaard too saw that there is this running up against something and he referred to it in a fairly similar way (as running up against paradox). This running up against the limits of language is *ethics* . . . But the inclination, the running up against something, *indicates something*. St Augustine knew that already when he said: What, you swine, you want not to talk nonsense! Go ahead and talk nonsense, it does not matter![6]

In addition to these conversations, what gave Wittgenstein the final reason to return to philosophy was a lecture given by the Dutch mathematician L.E.J. Brouwer in Vienna in March 1928. Brouwer lectured on the foundations of mathematics and defended his own view, intuitionism, which was opposed to Frege's and Russell's logicism and Platonism. Brouwer argued that mathematics is not a branch of logic and does not consist of truths about some super-reality, which mathematicians discover (the way Columbus discovered America). Instead, mathematics is a creation of the human mind. Wittgenstein was much agitated after this lecture and spent three hours in a café discussing it with two members of the Vienna Circle. He sympathized with Brouwer's critique of logicism, but felt at the same time challenged by his views. It was after Brouwer's lecture that he resolved to return to Cambridge and do philosophy again.

In January 1929 Wittgenstein was back in Cambridge, where he was to stay, with short interruptions, for seven years. 'Well, God has arrived. I met him on the 5.15 train', Keynes wrote to a friend. At almost 40, Wittgenstein was re-admitted as a student to Trinity College and stayed in residence for the following two terms, having Ramsey, who was fifteen years his junior, as his official supervisor. Since he needed a degree in order to qualify for grants and academic jobs, he submitted the *Tractatus* as his PhD thesis. As if this was not unusual enough, in June he had a viva voce examination with none other than Moore and Russell, the very philosophers to whom he had explained and dictated parts of his book years ago. Now the roles were reversed, if only formally. The situation was described by Russell as the most absurd he ever experienced. The exam started with a casual chat between the friends. After a while Russell said to Moore: 'Go on, you've got to ask him some questions – you're the professor.' Some discussion about the *Tractatus* ensued, with Russell complaining about the supposed nonsensicality of the propositions of the book. Eventually, Wittgenstein ended the session by clapping his examiners' shoulders and saying 'Don't worry, I know you'll never understand it.'[7]

Wittgenstein started working on philosophy almost immediately after his arrival in Cambridge. He began to write down his thoughts in the first of the eighteen large-format manuscript volumes he was to complete by 1940, each amounting to 300 pages. First he tried to execute the programme of the *Tractatus*, for example, to determine what the postulated atomic objects might be. But he failed in this, as he acknowledged himself in 'Some Remarks on Logical Form', the only journal article he ever published, written in July 1929. This failure prompted him to look increasingly critically at his logical atomism and gradually to reject more and more of his old ideas, until he finally discarded the whole conception of language in the *Tractatus* and replaced it with a new one. This conception was given its ultimate formulation in his masterwork, the *Philosophical Investigations*, completed only in 1946 and published posthumously (see chapter Eight). The years 1929–32 laid the foundation for this new philosophy, although in this transitional period we find him toying with all kinds of other ideas.

In Cambridge, as elsewhere, Wittgenstein was inclined to solitude, although exchange with others was always vital for him, both intellectually and psychologically. Fortunately, there were enough brilliant minds around he could befriend. Russell was not teaching in Cambridge any more, but Moore was. More importantly there

Wittgenstein's friend, the left-wing Italian economist Piero Sraffa.

was Ramsey, who provided him with valuable critical feedback, 'to a degree which I am hardly able to estimate', as he later wrote in the preface of the *Philosophical Investigations*. Unfortunately, Ramsey died in January 1930 at the age of 26, a great loss for Wittgenstein and for British philosophy. There was, however, one disadvantage in the exchange with Ramsey: the latter was more interested in the details of a theory, not in the bigger picture. As Wittgenstein wrote a year after Ramsey's death: 'Ramsey was a bourgeois thinker . . . He did not reflect on the essence of the state . . . but on how *this* state might reasonably be organized. The idea that this state might not be the only possible one partly disquieted him and partly bored him.'[8]

A less 'bourgeois' and more 'Bolshevist' discussion partner was Piero Sraffa (1898–1983), a gifted Italian economist who was lecturing at King's College. Sraffa was a Marxist and friend of Antonio

Gramsci. Despite not being a philosopher, he was not afraid of challenging Wittgenstein head-on, unlike so many others. Indeed, Wittgenstein acknowledged that during his discussions with Sraffa he often felt like a tree robbed of its branches. Most of their exchange was about philosophy, although Sraffa also informed Wittgenstein, who disliked reading newspapers, about current affairs. Sraffa was, unlike Ramsey, interested in the broader picture and could help Wittgenstein see things in totally new ways. A famous incident illustrating Sraffa's impact on Wittgenstein occurred when they were travelling by train and discussing logic. Wittgenstein was defending the idea expressed in the *Tractatus* that all propositions must be pictures and must have the same logical form. In response to this Sraffa made the Neapolitan gesture of contempt that consists of brushing the underneath of one's chin with the finger-tips and asked: 'What is the logical form of *that*?' According to Wittgenstein, this incident broke the spell that had seduced him to believe for so long that propositions must have a uniform essence.[9] Language is embedded in our ways of life and does not have only one purpose or essence – an insight that became part and parcel of his later philosophy. Sraffa and Ramsey were the only two people who were mentioned and thanked in the Preface of the *Philosophical Investigations*.

Another important Cambridge friend was J. M. Keynes, who assisted in integrating Wittgenstein into the university's social life again, including the society of the Apostles, which he had left in disgust in 1913. Through his *Tractatus* Wittgenstein had become in the meantime a legendary figure and the Apostles were thrilled to welcome him back. Equally, he came in touch with the Bloomsbury group and possibly Virginia Woolf, although we find hardly any references to each other in their writings.[10] Wittgenstein, with all his monkish tendencies, did not feel comfortable in these circles, especially if women were present, in which case he chose not to discuss any serious matter, but made shallow conversation and shallow jokes. He once walked out from a lunch because sex was discussed in the company of women. Obviously he felt more at home with individual people, especially young men, if they struck a particular chord in him. A good example of this is Gilbert Pattison, an undergraduate who later became a chartered accountant in London. Pattison had no interest in philosophy or in tormenting himself with ethical questions. Nevertheless, he was a close friend of Wittgenstein for over ten years, since they shared a predilection for trivia and 'talking nonsense by the yard'. This involved watching Hollywood movies together at Leicester Square, ridiculing advertisements in magazines and shops, and exchanging silly letters, in which they would address each other with 'Dear Blood', sign with 'Yours bloodily' and generally use the word 'bloody' ad nauseam. Here is a typical exchange:

> Dear Gilbert, . . . It might interest you to hear that I've had a slight accident & broke a rib. I thought of having it removed & of having a wife made of it, but they tell me that the art of making women out of ribs has been lost. – Bloodily yours Ludwig

> Dear Blood. I will be at Piccadilly Circus at 5-40 p.m. on Thursday next, & I will also make all proper arrangements with Major Lyons for Saturday. It is quite useless to experiment with ribs unless they are the fifth (from the top). Were you playing football or merely carousing? I recently received a tin of Messrs Allenbury's mixture from an anonymous benefactor. Yours etc Gilbert[11]

Another Cambridge society whose meetings Wittgenstein regularly attended, as before the war, was the Moral Science Club, where he began to make younger friends and disciples. The sessions of the society soon became dominated by the still youthful-looking philosopher, so much so that some members of the older generation, like C. D. Broad, Professor of Moral Philosophy, stopped their attendance in protest against Wittgenstein regularly 'going through his hoops' while his followers 'wondered with a foolish look of praise'.[12] According to Monk, the reason why Wittgenstein chose predominantly young men as his disciples and friends was the fact that he preferred being surrounded by 'childlike innocence and first-class brains' than by stiff professors.[13] He was working on what he considered a revolutionary conception of philosophy and hoped that his new ideas would be better understood by the younger generation. His charisma was overwhelming and left a permanent mark on many of his pupils. As one of them, Desmond Lee, has pointed out, Wittgenstein was in this respect similar to Socrates; they both had a numbing and hypnotic effect on young men.[14] This effect was not always to the students' benefit. He demanded absolute loyalty and expected tolerance of his irascible character, while he was in no way tolerant towards others. As Mary Midgley puts it:

> People who go about treading on other people's toes are peculiarly unaware of what it is like to be trodden on, so that they are naturally much surprised when it happens to themselves . . . Tolerance was not in Wittgenstein's repertoire and he liked to remove it from other people's.[15]

Wittgenstein himself was not unaware of some of his flaws; he once said to a friend: 'Although I cannot give affection, I have a great need for it.' But was he also aware that his powerful personality could distort that of others? Since he despised academia and romanticized a 'simple' life, he convinced several students to give up their studies and take up a practical profession, much to the dismay of their parents. He even interfered in matters of life and death. Thus when one of his closest friends and pupils, Maurice Drury, was about to embark for D-Day in 1944, Wittgenstein gave him a piece of advice that was based on his own attitude to death in the First World War: 'If it ever happens that you get mixed up in hand-to-hand fighting, you must just stand aside and let yourself be massacred.' One may wonder whether he had any right to use his authority in such an irresponsible way. In all fairness, it should be mentioned that his friends probably would have not accepted such criticism. Drury himself has publicly disputed that Wittgenstein was a 'rather cantankerous, arrogant, tormented genius'. On the contrary, for Drury Wittgenstein was 'the most warm-hearted, generous, and loyal friend anyone could wish to have'.[16]

Another well-known Cambridge society was The Heretics. Wittgenstein seems to have attended only one of its sessions, in November 1929, but it was here that he presented what is his most accessible text, 'Lecture on Ethics' (posthumously published). It is also his only contribution to philosophical ethics, apart from the remarks at the end of the *Tractatus*. In this lecture he tried to counter the impression that he was a positivist and anti-religious thinker, as many of his readers thought, by stressing again that absolute values, for example, those that make an action such as murder evil, are not facts in this world, but transcendent. Consequently, there can be no science of ethics, since science deals with facts in the world. Absolute values can only be experienced. Any attempt to express them ends in nonsense. So far, so *Tractatus*. Where the lecture goes beyond the book is to give a veritable phenomenology of religious experience. He discusses three such experiences, namely those summarized by the phrases 'How extraordinary that anything should exist' (the wonder of the world), 'I am safe, nothing can injure me whatever happens' (absolute safety) and 'God disapproves of our conduct' (absolute guilt), but only to demonstrate that these very phrases are meaningless. He writes:

> We all know what it means in ordinary life to be safe. I am safe in my room, when I cannot be run over by an omnibus. I am

safe if I have had whooping cough and cannot therefore get it again. To be safe essentially means that it is physically impossible that certain things should happen to me and therefore it is nonsense to say that I am safe whatever happens. Again this is a misuse of the word 'safe' as the other example was of a misuse of the word 'existence' or 'wondering'.

And he concludes:

My whole tendency and, I believe, the tendency of all men who ever tried to write or talk Ethics or Religion was to run against the boundaries of language. This running against the walls of our cage is perfectly, absolutely hopeless. Ethics so far as it springs from the desire to say something about the ultimate meaning of life, the absolute good, the absolute valuable, can be no science. What it says does not add to our knowledge in any sense. But it is a document of a tendency in the human mind which I personally cannot help respecting deeply and I would not for my life ridicule it.[17]

Despite his continuing dislike of academic life, Wittgenstein decided to stay in Cambridge. However, since he was now without any income, he faced financial difficulties. For the year 1929–30 he received, with the help of his friends, a grant to continue his research and lecture on philosophical logic for two terms. When this temporary arrangement came to an end, a more durable solution had to be found. In the summer of 1930 he applied for a five-year research fellowship at Trinity College. The work he submitted for examination was a compilation of remarks from the manuscripts he had completed to date (published as *Philosophical Remarks* in 1964), and was evaluated by Russell and the mathematicians J. E. Littlewood and G. H. Hardy. Russell wrote in his recommendation:

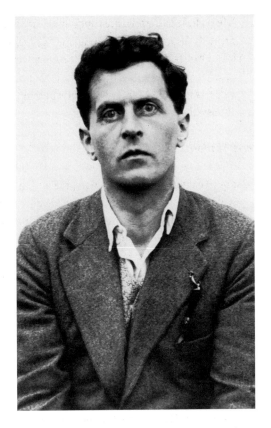

A college
photograph of
Wittgenstein at
Cambridge.

The theories contained in the work of Wittgenstein are novel,
very original and indubitably important. Whether they are true,
I do not know. As a logician who likes simplicity, I should wish
to think that they are not, but from what I have read of them I
am quite sure that he should have an opportunity to work them
out, since when completed they may easily prove to constitute a
whole new philosophy.[18]

The fellowship was granted. It brought Wittgenstein great relief
and allowed him to focus on philosophy for a prolonged period.

When asked by Richard Braithwaite under what title his first lectures should be announced, Wittgenstein, after remaining silent for a long while, finally replied that the subject would be philosophy. 'What else can be the title of the lectures but Philosophy.' This was to remain the title of all his lectures in Cambridge, save those for 1932–3, which were announced as 'Philosophy for Mathematicians'. Wittgenstein's 'career' as a lecturer lasted from 1930 to 1947, with the exception of 1936–8 and some of the war years. In the course of these years he lectured on a wealth of topics, including the nature of philosophy, the philosophy of logic and language, the intentionality of thought and language, the critique of metaphysics, solipsism and idealism, the philosophy of mathematics, sense data and private experience, cause and effect, aesthetics, religious belief and Freudian psychology. Fortunately, extensive student notes of some of these classes have survived. Wittgenstein's lectures soon became legendary and contributed to the aura of genius that already surrounded him. Over the years many students and colleagues attended them, for instance, Alice Ambrose, Elisabeth Anscombe, Max Black, Peter Geach, Norman Malcolm, G. E. Moore, Iris Murdoch, Rush Rhees, John Wisdom, Stephen Toulmin, Alan Turing,[19] Georg Henrik von Wright and many others. Several of his students were to become distinguished philosophers themselves, and it was through these pupils that Wittgenstein's new ideas were transmitted to the rest of Britain, and to the USA, Australia and the Scandinavian lands.

When he started lecturing in 1929 Wittgenstein was concerned that he had to switch from German to English, given that his manuscripts were all drafted in German, but this worry soon vanished, as Wittgenstein spoke excellent English with no accent. His lectures were informal and were quite unlike those in today's universities. They were held in his sparsely furnished rooms in Whewell's Court in Trinity College. But they made a lasting impression on anybody who attended them. Here is how Iris Murdoch, not a regular student, remembered Wittgenstein in retrospect:

He was very good-looking. Rather small, with a very, very intelligent, shortish face and piercing eyes – a sharpish, intent, alert face and those very piercing eyes. He had a trampish sort of appearance. And he had two empty rooms, with no books, and just a couple of deck chairs and, of course, his camp bed. Both he and his setting were very unnerving. His extraordinary directness of approach and the absence of any sort of paraphernalia were the things that unnerved people. I mean with most people, you meet them in a framework, and there are certain conventions about how you talk to them and so on. There isn't a naked confrontation of personalities. But Wittgenstein always imposed this confrontation on all his relationships. I met him only twice and I didn't know him well and perhaps that's why I always thought of him, as a person, with awe and alarm.[20]

Wittgenstein had no handouts, did not read from a script and did not even have notes, since he considered a lecture based on such 'material' artificial and stale. However, he did make much use of the blackboard. He was unforgiving with those who came late and did not allow casual attendance. As he said, 'My lectures are not for tourists.' Since he had thought about the problems involved for a long time, he only prepared for a few minutes before the lecture, recapitulating the previous week's results, then spoke freely and improvised, following one line of thought as it occurred to him there and then. His discourses, like his later writings, were illustrated with a wealth of vivid examples, striking metaphors and similes. He spoke with great authority and even when he struggled to find his words, or even remain silent for a long time, everybody had the impression that something important and groundbreaking was happening in their midst. 'During these silences, Wittgenstein was extremely tense and active. His gaze was concentrated; his face was alive; his hands made arresting movements; his expression was stern. One knew that one was in the presence of extreme serious-

The view from Wittgenstein's window in Trinity College, Cambridge.

ness, absorption, and force of intellect.'[21] Often he would conduct a monologue with himself and not let anybody interrupt him. Then again, he would engage somebody from the audience in a dialogue. His students were often frightened by him. Impatient and irascible, he forced them to formulate their thoughts in a precise way. Luckily, unlike in Austrian primary schools, there was no corporal punishment at Cambridge.

Wittgenstein's severity was connected, I think, with his passionate love of truth. He was constantly fighting with the deepest philosophical problems. The solution of one problem led to another problem. Wittgenstein was uncompromising; he had to have *complete* understanding. He drove himself fiercely. His whole being was under a tension. No one at the lectures could fail to perceive that he strained his will, as well as his intellect, to the utmost. This was one aspect of his absolute, relentless honesty. Primarily, what made him an awesome and even terrible person, both as a teacher and in personal relationships, was his ruthless integrity, which he did not spare himself or anyone else.[22]

Wittgenstein was rarely satisfied with his lectures. He would sometimes exclaim 'I'm just too stupid today!' or 'You have a dreadful teacher!' So exhausted and disgusted was he by his lectures that after class he often rushed off to the cinema to watch Hollywood movies, especially Westerns, sitting in the front row to disconnect himself fully from philosophy. He hardly watched any other movies. 'The typical American film, naïve and silly, can – for all its silliness and even *by means* of it – be instructive. The fatuous, self-conscious English film can teach one nothing. I have often learnt a lesson from a silly American film.'[23] There are a few other reflections on film from the same period in his diaries:

> In one regard I must be a very modern person since the cinema has such an extraordinary beneficial effect on me. I cannot imagine any rest for the mind more adequate to me than an American movie. What I see & the music give me a blissful sensation perhaps in an infantile way but therefore of course no less powerful. In general as I have often thought & said a film is something very similar to a dream & thoughts of Freud are directly applicable to it.[24]

After lecturing for two years in a row, in 1931 Wittgenstein felt that he needed more time to focus on his manuscripts and was granted research leave for a year. Nevertheless, he continued to give unpaid classes to interested students in his rooms. He was extremely productive in this period; by the summer of 1932 he had completed the tenth volume of his new manuscripts. His overall project consisted in dismantling the philosophy of the *Tractatus* and replacing it with his new ideas on the nature of language, logic and mathematics (see chapter Eight). He had also been cooperating, since 1929, with Friedrich Waismann on a book-length systematic presentation of his main ideas, announced as *Logic, Language, Philosophy*. The book was Schlick's idea. It was to be written by Waismann in a lucid and accessible style, thus contrasting with Wittgenstein's oracular writing. Waismann met Wittgenstein on many occasions, mainly during the latter's holidays in Austria, but the book was doomed, because Wittgenstein's philosophy was undergoing profound and unforeseeable changes, which made him periodically reject Waismann's drafts. As Waismann acknowledged, '[Wittgenstein] has the marvellous gift of always seeing everything as if for the first time. But I think it's obvious how difficult any collaboration is, since he always follows the inspiration of the moment and demolishes what he has previously planned.'[25] When Schlick, the *spiritus rector* of the project, was murdered by a disgruntled student in Vienna in 1936, Wittgenstein abandoned it. It was nevertheless completed by Waismann, and finally published in 1965 as *The Principles of Linguistic Philosophy*. The book remains one of the most readable introductions to Wittgenstein's thinking.

In 1931 Wittgenstein also worked on a series of remarks about James Frazer's monumental study in comparative anthropology and religion, *The Golden Bough* (12 volumes, 1911–15). The study was, despite its enormous scholarship, typical of the positivism at the turn of the century insofar as it took the myths of so-called primitive people to be primitive indeed, namely primitive science. According to Frazer, myth and magic are based on false beliefs. They are superstitions about natural phenomena, which were overcome in the West through the scientific revolution. Wittgenstein started reading the first volume of Frazer's book with Drury, but they did not get very far, since Wittgenstein stopped frequently to express his disapproval. His main contention was that Frazer was not attempting to *understand* primitive myths, but to give a merely genetic explanation of their historical origins (and even that explanation was mistaken). But this is to miss the actual meaning of the myths, their depth, their similarity to our own mythical and metaphysical ways of thinking. Frazer's explanations of primitive practices are more primitive than the practices themselves, Wittgenstein contended. In reality, '[a]ll religions are wonderful', he said to Drury, 'even those of the primitive tribes.'

> Frazer's account of the magical and religious views of mankind is unsatisfactory: it makes these views look like *errors*. Was Augustine in error, then, when he called upon God on every page of the *Confessions*? . . . But – one might say – if he was not in error, surely the Buddhist holy man was – or anyone else – whose religion gives expression to completely different views . . . The very idea of wanting to explain a practice – for example, the killing of the priest-king – seems wrong to me. All that Frazer does is to make them plausible to people who think as he does. It is very remarkable that in the final analysis all these practices are presented as, so to speak, pieces of stupidity. But it will never be plausible to say that mankind does all that out of sheer stupidity.[26]

> Burning in effigy. Kissing the picture of one's beloved. That is *obviously not* based on the belief that it will have some specific effect on the object which the picture represents. It aims at satisfaction and achieves it. Or rather: it *aims* at nothing at all; we just behave this way and then feel satisfied . . . The same savage, who stabs the picture of his enemy apparently in order to kill him, really builds his hut out of wood and carves his arrow skilfully and not in effigy . . . What a narrow spiritual life

on Frazer's part! As a result: how impossible it was for him to conceive of a life different from that of the England of his time! Frazer cannot imagine a priest who is not basically a present-day English parson with the same stupidity and dullness . . . Frazer is much more savage than most of his savages.[27]

It was soon after he resumed his public lectures in the academic year 1932–3 that Wittgenstein met Francis Skinner, a 20-year-old undergraduate in mathematics, the most promising of his year. He was good-looking, shy, gentle, bright, all features Wittgenstein found attractive, and within a short time Francis became a constant companion, an utterly devoted pupil and collaborator. How much Wittgenstein came to love Skinner can be gathered from the fact that the manuscript (*Philosophical Remarks*) on which Wittgenstein was working at the time contained the specification that the book should be published with the dedication 'To Francis Skinner'. There is a parallel here to David Pinsent, since the *Tractatus* was dedicated to the latter. But while David had not reciprocated Wittgenstein's feelings, Francis did. A few months after they met they started exchanging affectionate letters and addressed each other by their first names (which in those days had a greater significance than today). Thus in December 1932 Francis wrote: 'I am glad to read that you think about me. I think about you a lot.' When Wittgenstein was away during the summer vacation, Francis wrote: 'I feel much further away from you, and am longing to be nearer you again.'[28] From reading the letters one gets the impression that the infatuation or at least frankness was greater on Francis' side. He was so completely enamoured with Ludwig, so eager to please him, that he gave up his course in mathematics and slavishly devoted himself to the work of his older friend. Wittgenstein, on the other hand, needed this kind of attention and devotion, and the presence of the younger man suited him, making him calmer and more at ease with himself, as was observed by others. The relationship was asymmet-

Wittgenstein with his close friend Frank Skinner in Cambridge.

rical not only in an emotional but also in a philosophical respect, since Wittgenstein used his companion, whose official supervisor he was, not so much to discuss his ideas, but rather to record them. For three years they worked intensely, preparing Wittgenstein's book for publication, and Wittgenstein dictated to him and a few other close pupils several texts, including the so-called *Blue Book* (1933–4) and *Brown Book* (1934–5), the former consisting of lectures that can be read as an accessible introduction to his later philosophy. Valuable notes of Wittgenstein's lectures were also taken by Skinner.

How soon the relationship became intimate is difficult to tell, but intimate it did become. There is evidence of their love from later years. In letters from 1936 Francis speaks repeatedly about it. 'I think of you a lot and of our love for each other. This keeps me going and gives me cheerfulness and helps me to get over despondency.'[29] There are also encoded entries in Wittgenstein's diaries from 1937–8 which mention Ludwig's sensual feelings for his friend.[30] These passages also reveal that Wittgenstein felt guilty about these feelings. Here is one such intimate passage:

Masturbated last night. Pangs of conscience. But also the conviction that I am too weak to resist the impulse and temptation when certain images enter my mind, and I am not able to take refuge in other ones. And only *yesterday* evening I had thought about the necessity of the purity of my development! (I was thinking about Marguerite and Francis.)[31]

Note that Wittgenstein mentions Marguerite Respinger in this context as well. As Ray Monk has pointed out, it is a distortion to say, as the popular cliché has it, that Wittgenstein was tormented by his homosexuality, or at least solely by it.[32] Rather, he was troubled by sexuality as such, since it undermined the possibility of becoming the kind of self-controlled and chaste person he wanted to be. This is related to his belief in the sharp Weiningerian distinction between love and sex. Plausible as this explanation is, it is difficult to assume that the cause of his troubles with sex originated solely in Weininger's writings and would haunt him even in his mid-forties. Not even Wittgenstein was that cerebral. Rather, it is more likely that Weininger's theory brought out a basic insecurity about sex, which troubled him especially when it interfered with love, which he valued above all things. While the diary passages about sex are rare, tight-lipped and guilt-ridden, those concerning love and friendship are more explicit and at times even serene. Witness the following passage written towards the end of his life in connection with his feelings for another young man, Ben Richards:

Love is a *joy*. Maybe joy with pain, but joy nevertheless. If the joy is missing or it shrinks to a tiny flame, then love will be missing . . . *Love* is connected to one's nature . . . Love is that pearl of great value which one holds to the heart, which one does not exchange for *anything* else, which one deems the most valuable thing. It *shows* one, when one has it, the meaning of great value itself. One learns what this means: to know the value. One learns what this means: to separate precious metal from the rest.[33]

In 1936 both Wittgenstein's fellowship and Skinner's graduate course came to an end. Wittgenstein had decided to quit academia again and he convinced his friend to do the same. Skinner volunteered to fight in the Spanish Civil War, but was turned down. Skinner's other preferred profession, a doctor, was one Wittgenstein envisaged for himself in these years. But due to shortage of funding, Skinner eventually settled for Wittgenstein's second, more Tolstoyan choice: being a factory worker. It was as if Wittgenstein was trying to recreate his younger self in Francis. Understandably, the young man's parents, knowing how promising his initial results in mathematics had been, were outraged and completely opposed to this choice and Wittgenstein's influence on their son. But Francis accepted only Ludwig's authority, and thus entered an apprenticeship as a mechanic at a company in Cambridge, which did not make him very happy. They saw each other more sporadically in 1936–7, since Wittgenstein was mostly away from England, but in 1938, when Wittgenstein returned to Cambridge, they lived together as a couple in Francis's flat in Cambridge. However, by 1939 the relationship had deteriorated, maybe because of the too-intense closeness between the two. The philosopher sought to distance himself, both emotionally and physically, from the overly devout love of the younger man. The relationship was finally brought to a tragic end when Skinner died in 1941, at the age of 29, of poliomyelitis. Wittgenstein was devastated. At Francis's funeral he was described as behaving like a 'frightened wild animal'.[34] A few months later he wrote in his diary:

> Think a lot about Francis, but always only with remorse over my lovelessness; not with gratitude. His life and death seem only to accuse me, for I was in the last two years of his life very

often loveless and, in my heart, unfaithful to him. If he had not been so boundlessly gentle and true, I would have become *totally* loveless towards him.[35]

And in 1946 he wrote:

Ask yourself this question: when you die, who will grieve for you; and how *deep* will this grieving be? Who is grieving for Francis; how deeply do I grieve for him, I, who have more reason for grieving than anybody else? Does he *not* deserve that somebody grieves for him for the rest of his life? If anybody, then he does. Here one is inclined to say: God will save him and give him what a bad person has denied him.[36]

Apart from his relationship with Skinner and his philosophical progress, there were few other significant developments in Wittgenstein's life up to 1938. He was mostly dedicated to his philosophy and in this was extraordinarily productive. His mode of composition was as before. He entered remarks in notebooks, then compiled them in more polished form in large manuscripts or in dictation to a typist. Countless manuscripts and typescripts were thus completed, but because he was never satisfied with them, he constantly redrafted and reworked them, cutting out and repositioning individual remarks, sometimes agonizing over individual phrases and sentences, all to find 'the liberating word'. The most important work from this period is the so-called *Big Typescript*, named posthumously and published only very recently in English. This is a long typescript of some 750 pages, which he dictated to a typist while on holiday in Hochreit in 1933, and which embodied the fruits of his intense work since 1929. One third of it deals with philosophy of mathematics – a clear sign of the importance he attached to the topic. The rest deals with the essence of language, the philosophy of psychology and the nature of philosophy – in other words the main interests of his later work. The *Big Typescript* was evidently intended as the draft of a major book, containing chapter headings and a table of contents, but upon completion he was so dissatisfied that he called it a 'rubbish bin', attempting to redraft it at least three times. This is surely a misjudgement, since the text is philosophically extremely rich. Many remarks in his later masterwork, *Philosophical Investigations*, are adopted straight from it. The *Big Typescript* can be read as an independent book and is at times more transparent and explicit than the *Philosophical Investigations*, containing illuminating reflections that he did not exploit later, for reasons nobody will ever know. After discarding the *Big Typescript*, Wittgenstein worked on other attempts to formulate his new philosophy and, finally, in 1936, he started a manuscript that would lead to the *Philosophical Investigations*.

The only other significant events of these years were his journey to the Soviet Union in 1935 and his stay in Norway in 1936. Both can be seen as attempts to flee from his academic existence in Cambridge. Moreover, his attraction to the Soviet Union was based on escaping the West, a civilization he perceived as doomed and decadent. Wittgenstein had read Keynes's essay *A Short View of Russia*. Although Keynes was very critical of the economic system in the Soviet state, he expressed admiration for the Communists' ability to found a quasi-religious faith. This is what Wittgenstein was probably drawn to when reading Keynes's description – the prospect of a radically new life, of religious renewal on Tolstoyan terms. Wittgenstein's reasoning is not entirely transparent, however. For, as Ray Monk has pointed out, the Soviet Union in the 1930s was not Tolstoy's idyllic country but the Moloch of Stalin's Five Year Plans.[37] Was Wittgenstein also influenced by his surroundings? After all, in the early 1930s Cambridge was going through a communist frenzy. There were not only the Apostles, a playground and recruiting ground for Marxists, but also the Cambridge Communist Party and the Cambridge Communist Cell. There were people like the art historian Anthony Blunt and the under-graduate Kim Philby, who later formed the notorious spy-ring of the Cambridge Five. W. W. Bartley III has even alleged, without proof, that Wittgenstein was a recruiter of these spies. Last, but not least, Wittgenstein had several Marxist friends, such as Piero Sraffa, Nikolai Bakhtin, Fania Pascal and George Thompson. But it is unlikely that somebody as uncompromising as Wittgenstein could have been influenced by such an indoctrinated context.

Whatever sympathy Wittgenstein had for communism, it was probably not based on ideological reasons. He once said to Thompson, a classicist and member of the Communist Party, 'I am a Communist', but immediately added '*at heart*'. By contrast, to Fania Pascal, an Ukrainian philosopher settled in Britain, he spoke in such a deprecatory way about Marxist ideology that on one occasion he managed to outrage her. It seems that his aversion to anything doctrinal and organized affected not only his attitude to religion, but also to politics, and Marxism could not be excepted from this. An episode with Pascal confirms this:

> I had just been elected to the Cambridge Committee of the Friends of the Soviet Union and imparted the good news to the two of them. Wittgenstein told me firmly that political work was the worst possible thing for me to do; it would do me great harm. 'What you should do is to be kind to others. Nothing else. Just be kind to others.'[38]

Furthermore, the Marxist doctrine of social engineering did not fit well into Wittgenstein's overall world picture. As he wrote in 1930 in a projected preface to *Philosophical Remarks*, the spirit of modern civilization 'the expression of which is the industry, architecture, music, of present day fascism & socialism, is a *spirit that is alien & uncongenial* to the author'.[39] Note that Wittgenstein here places socialism next to fascism, not unlike a conservative thinker such as Martin Heidegger, who around the same time saw communism, fascism and even democracy originating from one and the same source, namely 'the universal rule of the will to power'.[40] Heidegger, perversely, joined the party lines of National Socialism. Since joining a party and ideology was not a route available to Wittgenstein, the only explanation we can find for his attraction to the Soviet Union is his romantic longing for a new life – paired with political naïvety and ignorance about the situation in the Soviet Union.[41]

Thus in the early 1930s Wittgenstein considered settling in Russia for good, ideally with Francis, where they would take up medical training or work as simple labourers. He even learned Russian to this end (which enabled him to read Dostoevsky in the original). Provided with contacts to Soviet officials and academics through Keynes, Wittgenstein finally went on a reconnaissance trip in September 1935. We do not know much about this journey. He stayed for two weeks, travelled to Leningrad and Moscow, and met many people, especially scientists and Marxist philosophers. They seemed to misunderstand the purpose of his stay; they offered him academic posts, in one case a professorship at Kazan University (where his idol Tolstoy had studied in 1844!), but not the simple work he sought for himself and Francis. When he introduced himself to Sophia Janovskaya, a philosopher from Moscow, she exclaimed 'What, not the great Wittgenstein?' For a while after his return from Russia Wittgenstein toyed with the idea of accepting the academic posts. However, his enthusiasm for the Soviet Union was gone. Why exactly, we do not know, since he remained almost completely silent about his experience, apparently so as not to have his name used for anti-Soviet propaganda. A plausible explanation could be that he was simply disillusioned by the realities of the Soviet Union, given that he now compared Soviet life to being a private in an army.[42] But this is at odds with the fact that even after his trip Wittgenstein did not make much of the justified criticism of Stalin's totalitarianism. 'Tyranny doesn't make me feel indignant', he said to Rush Rhees. He continued to express his sympathy with the Soviet experiment, presumably because it seemed to be so different from the decaying West, indeed even after the show trials during the Great Purge of 1936, not to mention the organized mass starvation of millions of Ukrainian peasants in the early 1930s. As late as 1939 he said to Drury: 'People have accused Stalin of having betrayed the Russian Revolution. But they have no idea of the problems that Stalin had to deal with; and the dangers he saw threatening Russia.'[43] The irony is that Stalin himself cited such 'problems' and 'dangers' to justify his Gulag camps. This understanding for the mass-murderer Stalin is incomprehensible, if we are to take Wittgenstein's otherwise firm ethical commitments seriously. At least he did not make a fool of himself publicly like other intellectuals in Britain, for instance George Bernard Shaw, who in 1934 described Stalin as the most candid and honest man, and the Soviet people as well-fed – just when they were suffering the most terrible famines.[44]

Wittgenstein's fellowship at Trinity was extended for one more year and finished with the summer term of 1936, which left him without any income and again with the feeling of being an outcast. He decided to go to Norway, as in 1913, to finish his work, but possibly also to get away from the slightly suffocating relationship with Francis. At the end of August he was again in his old house near Skjolden. For well over a month he attempted to rework his latest manuscript (the *Brown Book*), but eventually became exasperated with it and gave up, considering the result 'worthless', 'boring and artificial'. He then started a new version of his book, which, as mentioned earlier, later made up a significant portion of the *Philosophical Investigations*. Once again, Norway proved to be the right environment for him to do serious philosophical work. But it also proved to be the right place to deal with his sins. Feeling that he was morally depraved, he wrote up a very personal confession, which he distributed among friends and family. Among the addressees were Skinner, Moore, Drury, Engelmann and Pascal. We do not know exactly what the confession contained, since most of his intimates never revealed anything about it. From Pascal we know that it dealt with Wittgenstein's denial of his Jewishness and his maltreatment of a pupil during his time as a schoolteacher. According to another source it also dealt with his sexuality.

Apart from several visits to Vienna and Cambridge, Wittgenstein stayed in Norway until Christmas 1937. There is a kind of romantic cult surrounding Wittgenstein's trips to Norway,[45] but in reality his stays were always accompanied by loneliness and despair. This was particularly true this time around. The thought of having to live on his own in his hut frightened him so much that for a while he chose to live in the house of Anna Rebni, an old woman he knew from the pre-war years. This anxiety gave him reason to reflect, once again, on his ethical standing. His impression was that, despite the personal confession he had written only the previous year, he was losing grip of himself again. He felt weak, shabby, depressed, seeing his own life as a problem. To use a phrase by Flaubert: his life was not 'dans le vrai'. And this brought him to reflect on religious faith again. This time he described himself as irreligious, for 'a man who lived rightly won't experience the problem [of life] as *sorrow*'. He admitted to not understanding the Christian faith. In February 1937 he wrote: 'Let me confess this: After a difficult day for me I kneeled during dinner today & prayed & suddenly said, kneeling & looking up above: "There is no one here." That made me feel at ease as if I had been enlightened in an important matter.'[46]

This passage, written in code, may be seen as a turning point in his attitude to religion. Clearly, the religious fervour of his former years had vanished. As he later said of his Catholic friends: 'I could not possibly bring myself to believe all the things that they believe.' In the strict sense of the word he was probably no longer religious. But in a sense there were still elements of religiosity in him. After all, he was conscious that he was living a life of sin and sorrow, a consciousness that in his earlier 'Lecture on Ethics' he had described as one of the three basic religious experiences. And there were still moments when he found the Christian faith attractive. Concerning this there is an intriguing passage in his diary from December 1937. He was on the ship returning from Skjolden to Bergen and came, while reading the Bible, across a passage in Corinthians 12:3: 'No man can say that Jesus is the Lord, but through the Holy Ghost.' While he agreed with this passage, because he felt that talk about Jesus as the Lord coming to judge him was meaningless to him, he also wrote:

> What inclines even me to believe in Christ's resurrection? I play as it were with the thought. – If he did not rise from the dead, then he decomposed in the grave like every human being. *He is dead & decomposed*. In that case he is a teacher, like any other & can no longer *help*; & we are once more orphaned & alone. And have to make do with wisdom & speculation. It is as though we are in a hell, where we can only dream & are shut out from heaven, roofed in as it were. But if I am to be REALLY redeemed, – I need *certainty* – not wisdom, dreams, speculation – and this certainty is faith. And faith is faith in what my *heart*, my *soul*, needs, not my speculative intellect. For my soul, with its passions, as it were with its flesh & blood, must be redeemed, not my abstract mind. Perhaps one may say: Only *love* can believe the Resurrection.[47]

Wittgenstein's attitude to faith was to be an ambivalent one from now on, not that of a believer, but not that of an atheist either. It was, at times, a more exploring, indeed philosophical attitude. All talk about the ineffable and the Higher was dropped (as was his distinction between saying and showing). Not speaking from the inner perspective of the mystic any more, he was now able to look at religion as such, its function in human life, at the role of religious beliefs in people's lives. This decidedly anthropological stance became explicit in three lectures he gave on religious belief when he returned to Cambridge in 1938. What we know about these lectures is based only on notes by his students, but even so they give insight into his ideas on a topic that always preoccupied Wittgenstein, although he wrote very little on it.[48] In these lectures he sets out to defend religion against the attack under which it has come in modern times, especially through the rise of science. Religion is radically different from science and therefore does not stand in competition with it. In particular, religious statements are not empirical statements or theories about the (after-) world competing with scientific ones. They are not held on the basis of evidence, as is for instance some hypothesis about our galaxy, and it is therefore a grave mistake to treat them on a par with scientific theories, as *both* atheists and certain theologians do. The physicist who rejects the existence of God or the Christian doctrine of the Resurrection because there is no evidence for it *and* the theologian who accepts God's existence on the basis of supposed evidence (or even 'proofs') are making the same mistake. Rather, religious beliefs, and notions such as 'God', 'resurrection', 'sin', etc. have no theoretical function at all. They only crystallize primordial ways of life, and are in this sense secondary. 'the *words* you utter or what you think as you utter them are not what matters, so much as the difference they make at various points in your life . . . *Practice* gives the words their sense.'[49] Religious statements express an attitude to life as a whole, for example, guilt, and only have meaning with reference to a certain form of life, to certain existential experiences. Note that religious statements now are described as having a meaning, while in his earlier philosophy he had dismissed them as meaningless. 'A *religious question* is either a question of life and death or it is (empty) babble. This language-game, one might say, gets played only with questions of life and death. Much like the expression "Ouch" only has a meaning as a cry of pain.'[50] A believer saying 'There will be a Judgement Day and this is when I shall be judged' is not like a meteorologist predicting that it will rain tomorrow. It is more like the cry for help of a man fighting for his life against a raging fire. His actions will not be based on forming hypotheses through judicious inductive inferences (e.g. 'Fire has hurt me in the past. This is a fire. Therefore this fire will hurt me now'), but on terror.[51] Religious beliefs and rituals express this terror, among other things (they also express awe for the fact of life, etc.). Since they are not based on opinions and hypotheses, there is nothing right or wrong about them, and believers are neither rational nor irrational.

> Consider someone in horrible pain, say when something particular is happening in his body, yelling 'Away, away!', even though there is nothing that he wishes away, – could one say now: *'These words are wrongly applied'*?? One wouldn't say such a thing. Equally, if, for example, he makes a 'defensive' gesture or rather falls upon his knees & folds his hands, one couldn't reasonably declare these to be *wrong* gestures. *This is just what he does* in such a situation. There can be no talk of 'wrong' here ... Apply this to prayer. How could one say of him who *must* wring his hands & beseech, that he is mistaken or in an illusion.[52]

There are several important consequences of Wittgenstein's reflections on religion. One is that there is no need for a proof for the existence of God, given the non-theoretical and non-cognitive status of statements about God. Another is the radical difference between scientific and religious statements, which implies that there can be no dialogue between scientists and believers. Religious discourse is fundamental and irreducible, and thus incommensurable with scientific discourse. (This also implies that a scientist *can* be religious.) It follows that there can be no science of religion, no scientific explanation of religious beliefs in terms of other factors, such as sexuality (Freud), society (Marx) or evolution (Darwin). All we can and should do is describe religious life, not explain it. Wittgenstein's understanding of religion stands in sharp opposition to contemporary attempts to explain religion away, like now fashionable neuroscientific theories based on 'brain scanning'. It has affinities with other non-reductive investigations into the nature of religion that emerged in the early twentieth century, for example, Rudolf Otto's or Mircea Eliade's phenomenologies of religion. Last but not least, given the non-theoretical status of religious statements, one cannot use rational discourse to make somebody believe in them. But what would make one believe in a religious doctrine then? On this, Wittgenstein does not say anything substantial, indeed presents himself as agnostic:

> Suppose someone said: 'What do you believe, Wittgenstein? Are you a sceptic? Do you know whether you will survive death?' I would really, this is a fact, say, 'I can't say. I don't know,' because I haven't any clear idea what I'm saying when I'm saying, 'I don't cease to exist,' etc.[53]

However, towards the end of his life we find the following intriguing entry in his diary:

> Life can educate one to a belief in God. And *experiences* too are what bring this about; but I don't mean visions and other forms of sense experience which show us the 'existence of this being', but, e.g., sufferings of various sorts. These neither show us God in the way a sense impression shows us an object, nor do they give us rise to *conjectures* about him. Experiences, thoughts, – life can force this concept on us.[54]

So perhaps 'life' itself gives reasons to be a believer. But it is characteristic of Wittgenstein in his later years that he did not say that life has educated *him* to believe in God. At least, he continued to take religion immensely serious and also to pray occasionally. As he confessed to Drury: 'I am not a religious man but I cannot help seeing every problem from a religious point of view.'[55]

7

Professorship and Wartime, 1939–47

The rise of Hitler and Nazism in Germany throughout the 1930s was something even an apolitical person like Wittgenstein could not ignore. As George Thompson saw it, Wittgenstein became politically aware during the 1930s, at least in so far as he was 'alive to the evils of unemployment and fascism and the growing danger of war'.[1] But the black cloud slowly gathering over European civilization was of little personal concern for him. There is at any rate no significant mention of the Nazis in his diaries or letters of the time. However, things changed dramatically in 1938, the year in which Austria, his native land, was annexed into Greater Germany. At the turn of the previous year, Wittgenstein was, as every year, visiting his family in Vienna for the Christmas vacation. They gathered around the Christmas tree and sang the Austrian national anthem, feeling, as Hermine put it in retrospect, that it was 'the most lovely Christmas ever'.[2] It was also to be their last Christmas together. Wittgenstein went on to visit his former pupil Drury, who was training as a psychiatrist in Dublin (after Wittgenstein had convinced him to give up his studies at Cambridge). Wittgenstein was very interested in Drury's work and was allowed to visit and talk to mentally ill patients a few times per week. From Dublin he followed anxiously the developments in Austria, asking Drury about the news every evening. He was also in correspondence with Ludwig Hänsel, who gave him a detailed description of the political situation in Austria, telling him about 'triumphal rallies of the [Austrian] Nazis' taking place all over the country. On 12 March 1938 Drury informed Wittgenstein about the *Anschluss*. Wittgenstein and his family were now no longer Austrians, but Germans or, more precisely, German Jews, which made them subject to the racist Nuremberg Laws. Wittgenstein wrote on the same day in his diary: 'What I hear about Austria disturbs me. Am unclear what I should do, whether to go to Vienna or not.' And a few days later, contemplating the various external and internal dilemmas, including his own Jewishness, involved in possessing a *Judenpaß*, he wrote:

> I am now in an extraordinarily difficult situation . . . I have become a German citizen. That is for me a frightful circumstance, for I am now subject to a power that I do not in any sense recognise. The German citizenship is like a hot iron which I would have to constantly carry with me . . . What would now be the difference between a *Judenpaß* and the old Austrian passport? Why should this one, but not the other one, burn in the pocket? Is it because of the stigma associated with it in Austria? You will live in Austria with your relatives and not notice it; and the same abroad. In spite of this, I sense that this association will be a permanent burden on me. Partly because my situation won't be stated in clear and simple terms . . . But also because I could not work in Austria; and I *must* work in order to live, I mean: to keep myself sane . . . But one could say: Why don't you want to endure all this for your family? Possible imprisonment in Austria, unemployment, separation from your dearest friend, disquiet and anxiety before losing freedom, a crooked inclination in all directions? Why not assume it? How would I have to position myself to be able to assume it? I am afraid, I am not capable of this position.[3]

Nevertheless, he wrote to his family, offering to come to Vienna. He also contemplated changing his nationality and wrote to Piero

Sraffa in Cambridge for advice. Sraffa urged him '*you must not go to Vienna*', for he would not have been allowed to leave the country again. Fortunately, Wittgenstein complied. Within days he decided to renounce his Austrian citizenship, accepting that he would be an immigrant from now on. 'But the thought of leaving my people alone is dreadful.'[4] On Sraffa's advice he first sought permanent employment with the university, asking for Keynes's support:

The thought of acquiring British citizenship had *occurred* to me before; but I have always rejected it on the ground: that I do not wish to become a sham-english-man (I think you will understand what I mean). The situation was however entirely changed for me now. For now I have to choose between two new nationalities, one of which deprives me of *everything*, while the other, at least, would allow me to work in a country in which I have spent on and off the greater part of my adult life, have made my greatest friends and have done my best work.[5]

With Keynes's assistance Wittgenstein was appointed to a university lectureship. He then applied for naturalization, which was granted to him only one year later, in June 1939. More worrisome was the situation of his family. Since in the eyes of the Nazi authorities only one of Wittgenstein's grandparents was 'Aryan', Ludwig and his siblings all counted as Jews. Initial attempts by the family to renegotiate their racial status and prove that at least one more grandparent was an 'Aryan' failed. Paul Wittgenstein eventually left Austria and settled in New York. Margarete already lived in America with her husband. But Hermine and Helene refused to leave their native country until it was too late. With Margarete's help they procured false Yugoslav passports to get over to Switzerland, but all three sisters were soon arrested and spent a few nights in prison. Fortunately, they were cleared of charges in the subsequent trial. But the danger was really only lifted when the

Wittgensteins struck a financial deal with the Nazis. As Jews they were forced to sign over most of their assets to the Reichsbank. But since most of the family fortune was deposited in funds in US banks, the Nazis needed the cooperation of the family to access this money. The negotiations were brought to completion in August 1939. Hermann Christian Wittgenstein was declared of 'German blood', which made all his grandchildren, including Ludwig and his sisters, into *Mischlinge* ('hybrids') of first degree. This status could be lost if they were to marry a Jewish person, but they were soon excepted even from this condition. In return, the Wittgensteins transferred a staggering 1.7 tons of gold to the Nazi state, no less than 2 per cent of Austria's gold reserves at the time. Ludwig, who was very worried about his family during this period, became involved in the negotiations as soon as he received his British passport, and travelled to Berlin, Vienna and even New York to help out with the transaction. One may wonder about the ethical implications of this deal. A vast fortune was given to the Nazi machine, which was soon to wreck millions of people's lives, just so that the two women's 'perverse desire to stay in Austria' could be satisfied. How could Wittgenstein, given his strict opposition to unethical compromises, justify such a transaction? However, his opposition to compromises primarily applied to his own life. Here others were involved, over whose actions he had no control. He entered the negotiations at a comparatively late stage, when his sisters had already decided to stay in Austria and compromise with the Nazis. He did not oppose their decision, as his brother Paul did (which led to serious tensions in the family), but the main responsibility was still his sisters'. Moreover, despite the totalitarian character of Hitler's regime in the late 1930s, the war and the Holocaust had not yet taken place. And even if they had, who would not have acted just like him in similar circumstances? Who would not have given any available sum to save his beloved ones? The deal with the Nazis did involve a moral dilemma, but its horns were straight from hell.

Despite the worries about his family, Wittgenstein continued to work on philosophy after his return to Cambridge in 1938. In the summer he prepared the material he had written in Norway for publication, and offered it to Cambridge University Press under the title *Philosophical Remarks*. It was the earliest version of the *Philosophical Investigations*. The edition was supposed to be bilingual, including the German original and an English translation provided by one of his pupils, Rush Rhees. Wittgenstein withdrew his manuscript from Cambridge University Press within a month, being dissatisfied with both the content and Rhees's translation. The main reason for attempting this publication was his growing dissatisfaction with the fact that since 1929 ideas connected to his new philosophy had been disseminated by his colleagues and pupils in a watered-down form. In 1932 he accused Rudolf Carnap of plagiarism in letters to Schlick, not entirely without justification, but in a much too ferocious manner. In 1933 he wrote a furious letter to *Mind*, protesting against the inaccurate description of his ideas in a rather innocuous article by Richard Braithwaite. In 1935 Alice Ambrose, a gifted pupil, incurred his wrath because she decided to publish an article summarizing his philosophy of mathematics. He tried to convince her to abandon its publication, but after both she and the editor of *Mind*, G. E. Moore, refused to do so, Wittgenstein resigned as Ambrose's PhD examiner and broke off all contacts with her.[6]

Rhees's translation was not completely worthless, however. In early 1939 Wittgenstein applied for the chair in philosophy recently vacated by Moore, and submitted it as a token of his work. He was convinced that he would not be elected because the Oxford philosopher R. G. Collingwood, whom he suspected of hostile sentiments, was on the election committee. But as C. D. Broad, who was personally not fond of Wittgenstein either, remarked at the time: 'To refuse the chair to Wittgenstein would be like refusing Einstein a chair of physics', a remark that apparently amazed Wittgenstein.[7] He was

elected professor on 11 February 1939. This was the highest professional distinction for an academic philosopher (and one denied to
other great thinkers, e.g., Schopenhauer and Frege), but it meant
little to him: 'having got the professorship is very flattering & all
that but it might have been very much better for me to have got a
job opening & closing crossing gates. I don't get a kick out of my
position (except what my vanity & stupidity sometimes gets).'[8]
He was to remain in the position till 1947.

His first lectures as a professor were on philosophy of mathematics (published in 1976), a topic on which he worked almost
exclusively during the entire war. A year later, in 1940, he gave
seminars on his *Philosophical Investigations* and on aesthetics. As
in his lectures on religious belief, he argued in those on aesthetics
against the idolatry of 'Science and the Scientist'.

> You might think Aesthetics is a science telling us what's beauti-
> ful – almost too ridiculous for words. I suppose it ought to
> include also what sort of coffee tastes well . . . The idea is that
> once we are more advanced, everything – all the mysteries of
> Art – will be understood by psychological experiments.
> Exceedingly stupid as the idea is, this is roughly it.[9]

Scientific experiments can provide us with statistical data about
what people treat as 'beautiful' etc., but such experiments do not
tell us what *is* beautiful and *why* people find it so. The difference is
similar to the one between causality and motivation. If I am asked
in court 'Why did you kill this man?', the appropriate answer will
be to indicate the motives of my action, for example, because the
man cheated in poker. An answer with reference to the internal
mechanisms in my brain or body during my action will be simply
ignored (if I am lucky and the court does not think I am mocking
them!). Equally, when I am asked 'Why do you find this sonnet
beautiful, the beginning of this fugue peculiar, this statue awesome,

etc.', it would be a mockery to say 'Because of this and that brain process!' or 'Because 70 per cent of my relatives do!' But what does then define aesthetic appreciation? Wittgenstein's answer is typical of his later philosophy: don't assume there *must* be a unique answer to this question. Aesthetic appreciation is a very complex phenomenon, Wittgenstein argues, indeed not *one* phenomenon, but an 'immensely complicated family of cases'. To be sure, in an entry from his later diaries Wittgenstein does venture to indicate a unique or at least central feature of art: 'We might say: art *discloses* the miracles of nature to us. It is based on the *concept* of the miracles of nature.'[10] But in his lectures Wittgenstein is more careful: what art is cannot be indicated by a singular definition, since there is not one single feature that unifies all our aesthetic experiences or all those things we treat as works of art. Hence, there can be no theory of art that subsumes everything under general laws and causal explanations. What we need in aesthetics are not theories and explanations, but (sympathetic) descriptions.

> The words we call expressions of aesthetic judgement play a very complicated role, but a very definite role, in what we call a culture of a period. To describe their use or to describe what you mean by a cultured taste, you have to describe a culture. What we now call a cultured taste perhaps didn't exist in the Middle Ages. An entirely different game is played in different ages. What belongs to a language game is a whole culture.[11]

By 1940 the Second World War was well under way and Wittgenstein, now a British citizen, was anxious to be involved in war work of some kind, being frustrated with his confinement to academic life, which he dreaded more than ever. For several years he had been friends with Gilbert Ryle (1900–1976), a philosopher with whom he shared many ideas and who later was to become one of Oxford's most prominent thinkers and editor of *Mind*. Gilbert Ryle introduced Wittgenstein to his brother, John Ryle, who had been professor of medicine in Cambridge, but was now working at Guy's Hospital in London. To John Ryle Wittgenstein said: 'I feel I will die slowly if I stay [in Cambridge]. I would rather take a chance of dying quickly.'[12] As in the First World War he wished to be placed 'where the bombs are falling'. It was the old will to feel alive in the face of great danger, to be pulled out of lethargy and depression by the presence of death. But there was also a genuine concern with his new homeland, as he told Drury:

> You have often heard me speak of my dislike of many features of English life. But now that England is in real danger, I realize how fond I am of her; how I would hate to see her destroyed. I have often said to myself that William the Conqueror got himself a very good bargain.[13]

In September 1941 Wittgenstein started working as a dispensary porter at Guy's Hospital, which was in a heavily blitzed area of the capital. However, for a while he continued to teach in Cambridge, delivering private classes at weekends. His wish to work in London in anonymity was respected, although most staff members knew who he was and addressed him as 'Professor Wittgenstein'. His salary was 28 shillings a week (roughly £46 today), a fraction of the several hundred pounds sterling he made as a professor in Cambridge, and his main task consisted of delivering drugs to the wards, although he apparently advised patients not to take them. A former co-worker remembers: 'after working here three weeks he came and explained how we should be running the place. You see he was a man who was used to thinking.'[14] Soon he transferred to the manufacturing department as a laboratory assistant, where one of his responsibilities was to mix ointments for skin treatment, a task at which he excelled.

On the whole, his time at the hospital did not lift Wittgenstein's mood. At 52 he felt old and worn-out. Moreover, he was heartbroken over Francis's death in October 1941. He made a few friends, including John Ryle and his wife Miriam, who took him for a weekend to their house in Sussex. When, in April 1942, he had a gall-stone removed from which he had suffered for years, Ryle held his hand during the operation – a peculiar event, since Wittgenstein, distrusting the surgeons, refused general anaesthetic and observed the whole process through special mirrors installed for him. In the hospital Wittgenstein also befriended Roy Fouracre, a colleague at the dispensary. The latter was a simple, good-humoured young man from Hackney, who had a calming effect on Wittgenstein. When Wittgenstein was in a state of agitation, Fouracre would calm him down by saying 'Steady, Prof'. As with Gilbert Pattison, there was no intellectual dimension to their friendship. Nevertheless, or maybe because of this, the 'Prof' stayed friends with Fouracre to the end of his life, and when the young man was sent to the Front in the Far East, Wittgenstein wrote him many light-hearted letters, urging him to come back soon so that they could 'talk nonsense by the yard' again. At the hospital he also met Naomi Wilkinson, a cousin of the Ryles, who organized gramophone recitals in which Wittgenstein participated with much interest.

It was during his time at the hospital that Wittgenstein started to preoccupy himself in more depth with Freudian psychology. In the years 1942–6 he had several conversations with Rush Rhees about Freud, of which Rhees took extensive notes.[15] This was not his first encounter with psychoanalysis. Not only did he know about Freud from his sister Margarete, but Wittgenstein himself had discussed psychoanalysis in his lectures on aesthetics in 1938. Back then he expressed his admiration for those *practical* aspects of Freud's work which he considered illuminating, for example, Freud's imaginative interpretations of jokes in *Jokes and Their Relation to the Unconscious* (1905). But his attitude to Freud's *theories* was highly critical. Not only did he disapprove of Freud's dogmatic reduction of dreams to purely sexual contexts, but he rejected the underlying principle of explanation that posits hidden causal mechanisms in the human psyche. In his view the main reason why people find Freud's 'theory' of the unconscious so plausible is the idol-worship of science in our culture, the overwhelming attraction of the scientific mode of thinking, of reducing everything to cause and effect. In making such a reduction, one thinks that one finds out what things 'really' are. Dreams 'really' are repressed sexual desires, actions 'really' are caused by childhood experiences, people 'really' chatter because they are sexually unfulfilled, etc. To stress what things 'really' are empowers the individual, makes him feel as a destroyer of the prejudices of other, more naïve humans. For, as Wittgenstein puts it, 'It is charming to destroy prejudice.'[16] In his conversations with Rhees he stressed again what he found appealing in Freud, such as certain interpretations of dreams, or the therapeutic, self-healing effects an interpretation of one's life in terms of Greek tragedy might have.

> Many people have at some period, serious troubles in their lives – so serious as to lead to thoughts of suicide. This is likely to appear to one as something nasty, as a situation which is too foul to be a subject of a tragedy. And it may then be an immense relief if it can be shown that one's life has the pattern rather of a tragedy – the tragic working out and repetition of a pattern which was determined by the primal scene.[17]

But Wittgenstein also stressed the dangers involved in accepting any monolithic, uniform explanation of what is 'really' taking place in the human soul. Freud claimed that his was a scientific theory, but according to Wittgenstein it was pseudo-scientific or at best pre-scientific. Psychoanalysis in fact consists in making sense of phenomena by speculation based on free association –

a method that is *prior* to the formation of scientific hypotheses. Through free association one could always find some 'hidden' meaning in any kind of phenomena, not just in dreams. Take some table with random objects on it, for example, some papers, pens, a mug, a phone, some books and CDs. None of them has been put there through your dream activity. Now fix your mind on some problem of major significance in your life. It would not be too difficult to connect the objects through some pattern in such a way that the whole arrangement could be seen as a visualization or interpretation of your problem. Horoscopes or the reading of tea leaves are based on this kind of 'method'. But this pattern-creating interpretation does not prove anything, especially not how things are 'in reality'. We have not given a scientific explanation of how the objects on the table are connected, but just superimposed a certain story by pressing each object into its scheme. This activity is similar to that of creating a myth. Indeed, Wittgenstein contends, Freud's stories are not scientific explanations, but actually new myths.[18] He writes:

> Take Freud's view that anxiety is always a repetition in some way of the anxiety we felt at birth. He does not establish this by reference to evidence – for he could not do so. But it is an idea which has . . . the attraction which mythological explanations have, explanations which say that this is all a repetition of something that has happened before . . . So it is with the notion of the unconscious also. Freud does claim to find evidence in memories brought to light in analysis. But at a certain stage it is not clear how far such memories are due to the analyst. In any case, do they show that the anxiety was necessarily a repetition of the original anxiety?[19]

> Freud has performed a great disservice with his phantastic pseudo-explanations (precisely because they are ingenious).

(Now any ass has these pictures available to use in 'explaining' symptoms of illness.)[20]

At Guy's Hospital Wittgenstein made the acquaintance of two doctors, Basil Reeve and R. T. Grant, who were doing research on so-called wound shock (or traumatic shock) often observed in the numerous air-raid casualties. Not being able to give a precise clinical definition to this notion, the doctors suggested eliminating the notion 'wound shock' and simply recording the various symptoms of the casualties in as much detail as possible. Wittgenstein became interested in this approach, for it bore obvious similarities to the idea expressed in a passage in Hertz's *Principles of Mechanics* that he had admired so much since his youth, that if we remove the problematic notion of force, 'our minds . . . will cease to ask illegitimate questions' (see chapter Two). When the research unit moved to Newcastle Wittgenstein was offered the position of laboratory assistant, which was not only paid better, but offered him the opportunity to carry out an intellectually more interesting task.

Wittgenstein transferred to Newcastle in April 1943, where he stayed till February 1944. He left his mark here, as everywhere. As a secretary remembers, Wittgenstein did not fit easily into the narrow social context. While in the morning he came down for breakfast in a bright and chatty mood, his British colleagues preferred to read the newspaper and not talk. In contrast, when they enjoyed dinner together every evening, he had his meal alone in his room. 'Prof. W. had difficulty in finding anywhere to live because as he had a foreign accent, looked a bit shabby & said he was a professor, most landladies were quite naturally suspicious.'[21] His only friend there was Dr Reeve. However, despite his social awkwardness, his research was very successful. He not only invented an improved device for recording pulse pressure and its relation to breathing depth and rate, but also had a hand in the conceptual distinctions drawn in the report on wound shock that was the final fruit of the research project (published in 1951). The device has been lost, but Wittgenstein's contribution is visible in Dr Grant's report:

> he has a keenly critical mind and in discussions of medical and physiological problems has proved a most helpful and stimulating colleague. He has undertaken observations on respiratory variations of blood pressure in man, devising his own experiments and apparatus. The results of his work so far are at variance with commonly accepted views and of considerable interest.[22]

Wittgenstein wrote hardly any philosophy in Newcastle, which increasingly frustrated him. His main goal was still to finish and publish *the* book he had been working on since his return to philosophy in 1929. The book had gone through many versions, manuscripts and typescripts, but none ever satisfied him. In September 1943, after compiling yet another typescript, Wittgenstein approached Cambridge University Press again, this time with the plan to publish the new book together with the *Tractatus* as *Philosophical Investigations of the Tractatus-Logico Philosophicus*. The reason for this edition was that in this way his new ideas could be 'properly illuminated by being set in opposition to and against the background of my former way of thinking', as he wrote in the Preface. Although the typescript was accepted by the publisher in January 1944, Wittgenstein was so dissatisfied with it that he soon retracted the offer. Incidentally, the idea of publishing the *Tractatus* next to the *Investigations* had come to him in the previous year, while re-reading his earlier book with the philologist Nikolai Bakhtin, brother of the famous Marxist philosopher Mikhail Bakhtin. Nikolai originated from the Russian nobility and had fought during the Russian Revolution on the side of the White Army, but had become a devout communist in England, while also keeping his Orthodox faith. Why Wittgenstein chose to re-read the *Tractatus* with a philologist we do not know, but maybe because he found it more fruitful to talk to a non-philosopher about his ideas. Also, Bakhtin had a very lively and flamboyant personality. Wittgenstein was fond of him precisely because they were so different. The philosopher was 'unusually happy and gay in [Bakhtin's] presence, and never dropped him as easily as he did others'.[23] There might have been even some intellectual affinities. Bakhtin was a fierce opponent of uniformity and generality, of what he called 'the tyranny of abstract ideas and dogmas over life', which he saw embodied in Plato's philosophy, and endorsed instead Aristotle's preference for multiple distinctions, for 'continuous transitions of shades and qualities', which fitted well with Wittgenstein's new philosophical orientation.[24] However, to claim, as Terry Eagleton has done, that Wittgenstein's ideas were somehow related to the Marxist aesthetics of Mikhail Bakhtin via this broad affinity with brother Nikolai is to overlook subtle and not so subtle differences between Wittgenstein and Marxist thought.[25] 'Like primitive peoples, we are much more inclined to say "All these things, though looking different, are really the same" than we are to say "All these things, though looking the same, are really different."'[26]

Wittgenstein left Newcastle in February 1944 and after an intermezzo in Cambridge went to stay with Rhees in Swansea, where he had been in the previous two summers, and where he was to return several times in the following years.[27] Rhees, who was teaching philosophy at Swansea, had been one of his favourite pupils and was now one of his closest friends. Rhees's wife was a psychoanalyst of the Jungian school. Hence, Wittgenstein was in good company. He stayed in Swansea for almost half a year. It was here that he stopped working on philosophy of mathematics, a topic that not only had brought him to philosophy in the first place and made him return to it, but one that he had pursued tirelessly since 1929 (around half of his manuscripts from 1929 to 1944 are dedicated to it). Instead he now became interested in the philosophy of psychology (or philosophy of mind, as we would say today), and it is due to this shift of interest that the final manuscript of the *Philosophical Investigations* contains no philosophy of mathematics, but plenty of philosophy of psychology.[28]

In Swansea Wittgenstein worked intensively on his book, gave lectures at the university and made friends with several locals, as he found he could get along better with them than with people in England. 'The weather's foul, but I enjoy not being in Cambridge ... I feel much more often like smiling, e.g. when I walk in the street, or when I see children, etc.'[29] He lodged with several locals, including a Methodist minister, whom Wittgenstein teased with the remark that the numerous books in the house were not bought to be read, but to impress the flock. When the minister asked him whether he believed in God, Wittgenstein replied: 'Yes I do, but the difference between what you believe and what I believe may be infinite.'[30] Another incident involved one of the daughters of his neighbours, whom he befriended. He had supervised her progress in school. One day she came home in tears. Hearing that she had been failed, Wittgenstein replied 'Damn it all! We'll see about that!' and went in a rage to see the responsible teacher. He told the latter: 'I am stunned that you say she failed and I can tell you on authority that she *must* have passed.' And indeed, she had. The teacher checked the records and discovered that there had been a mistake.[31]

In October 1944 Wittgenstein was back in Cambridge, resuming his lecturing, mostly on philosophy of psychology, and continuing work on his book. He moved again into his old lodgings in Whewell's Court at Trinity College. During the Christmas vacation of 1944–5, which he spent in Swansea, he must have felt that he was nearing the end of his labours, for he drafted the final preface to the still unfinished book. It was, he wrote, 'the precipitate of philosophical investigations which have occupied me for the last sixteen years', adding grimly: 'It is not impossible that it should fall to the lot of this work, in its poverty and in the darkness of this time, to bring light into one brain or another – but, of course, it is not likely.'

Opus magnum: The typescript of Wittgenstein's *Philosophical Investigations*.

He was still not satisfied with what he had done. As he wrote to Norman Malcolm: '[The book] will probably disappoint you. And the truth is: it's pretty lousy. (Not that I could improve on it essentially if I tried for another 100 years.)'[32] Much of 1945 Wittgenstein spent trawling yet again through his numerous manuscripts, selecting further remarks and even adding new material. The final typescript of what we now call 'Part 1' of the *Philosophical Investigations* was completed in 1945–6, but even then Wittgenstein could not bring himself to publish it, and minor emendations were added to the manuscript over the following years.

'The darkness of the time' Wittgenstein was alluding to was indisputable; he was, after all, writing his preface towards the end of a war that had brought total devastation to the world, killing over 32 million civilians alone. But Wittgenstein did not have only the war in mind and, indeed, when it was over in August 1945, he saw no reason to join in the celebrations of victory, as he was appalled by what he considered 'the triumphant beastliness of the Allies in Germany & Japan'. Already during the war he had written: 'Things will be terrible when the war is over, whoever wins. Of course, very terrible, if the Nazis won, but terribly slimy if the Allies win.'[33] And after the ceasefire:

> Perhaps I ought to feel elated because the war is over. But I'm not. I can't help feeling certain that this peace is only a truce. And the pretence that the complete stamping out of the 'aggressors' of this war will make this world a better place to live in, as a future war could, of course, only be started by them, stinks to high heaven &, in fact, promises a horrid future.[34]

It may well be that the press reports about food shortages in Germany and Austria were one reason for his dismissal of the peace and the Allies, as Ray Monk suggests.[35] But surely, compared to anything the Axis had done in its occupied territories, the Allies were an incomparably more humane force, at least the Western ones. No horrid future was awaiting Western Europe (and Japan). On the contrary: the Marshall Plan was soon implemented by the US, leading to democracy and wealth in Germany and Austria. A terribly slimy and horrid future was awaiting only Eastern Europe, where the Soviet Union, Wittgenstein's erstwhile land of dreams, was about to install its iron rule. So what motivated his criticism? It was not so much the immediate events, but his old Spenglerian pessimism about the prospects of modern Western societies, driven by the spell of science and technology, whose advent, in his eyes, possibly marked the beginning of the end of humanity. He had, since his return to philosophy in 1929, grown increasingly adverse to *scientism*, the dogmatic application of scientific thinking to every realm of thought, be it language, mathematics, psychology, religion, anthropology or aesthetics. He had attempted to undermine this multifaceted idolatry of science by showing that important aspects of these disciplines are inaccessible to scientific theory-building. His philosophy was thus opposed not only to particular philosophical doctrines, but really to a much larger current, as he had made clear in the preface to the *Philosophical Remarks* (1930):

> This book is written for such men as are in sympathy with its spirit. This spirit is different from the one which informs the vast stream of European and American civilization in which all of us stand. That spirit expresses itself in an onwards movement, in building ever larger and more complicated structures; the other in striving after clarity and perspicuity in no matter what structure.

But even if we grant Wittgenstein this opposition to an exaggerated adoration of science in philosophy and culture – was he really justified to reject the entire modern Western civilization, with its many political, social and technical achievements? Can we really make sense of the apocalyptic desire expressed in the following diary entry?

> The hysterical fear over the atom bomb now being experienced, or at any rate expressed, by the public almost suggests that at last something really salutary has been invented. The fright at least gives the impression of a really effective bitter medicine . . . But perhaps this too is a childish idea. Because really all I can mean is that the bomb offers a prospect of the end, the destruction, of an evil, – our disgusting soapy water science . . . but who could say what would come *after* this destruction?[36]

A diversion from this gloomy mood arose when, in 1945, he met Ben Richards, a medicine student at King's College, Cambridge,

Wittgenstein with his friend Ben Richards in London.

who was over 35 years younger than Wittgenstein. Ben had similar qualities to Francis: he was kind, gentle, good-looking. Wittgenstein fell deeply in love with him. Since Francis there had been nobody else in his life, if we discount the case of Keith Kirk, a working-class colleague of Francis to whom Wittgenstein gave lessons in mechanics and mathematics in 1940. Wittgenstein was infatuated with Kirk, but kept his feelings secret and nothing ever developed. With Ben, however, the feelings seem to have been more mutual, leading to a relationship that lasted, with ups and downs, for several years.[37] Given that he felt old and worn-out this unexpected emotional outburst reinvigorated and inspired him, and made him forget about his daily worries, in particular the dreaded duties of his academic position. No doubt Ben's love was very precious to him, a 'great rare

gift' and a 'rare gem', as he described it in his diary. But this love
also led to new trouble, since it made him depend again on another
human being. It seems that he was now less capable than before
to bear the hazards of love, experiencing despair and anxiety at the
slightest uncertainty, such as a missing letter.

> Upset. No news from R. Every day I think about it and that I
> should find the right attitude towards this loss. Nothing seems
> more probable than that he has left me or is about to do it, and
> nothing, in a sense, more natural. And I feel that I must let all
> this happen as it is meant to, that I have done what I could and
> that now it is out of my hand. It is a mark of a *true* love that one
> thinks of what the *other* person suffers. For he suffers too, is also
> a poor devil.[38]

Containing painful reflections on his situation, his diary entries
of the time are reminiscent of the period when he was in love with
Marguerite Respinger. 'I am awfully depressed. Uncertain about
my whole future. My love story with Richards has totally exhausted
me. It has held me in its grip for the past nine months, almost like
madness.'[39] It is noteworthy, however, that unlike his relationship
to Francis, no pangs of conscience accompanied Wittgenstein's
love for Ben. Ray Monk has made the interesting conjecture that
Wittgenstein's attitude to sexuality had changed during the war.
He had, for most of his life, held onto Weininger's sharp distinction between sex and love. But by 1943 he had ceased to view
sex and love as incompatible, as an episode with Drury suggests.
Drury had recently visited Luxor Temple in Egypt and recounting
his journey to Wittgenstein he expressed his shock at a bas-relief
depicting Horus, the ancient god of the sky, with an erect phallus.
Wittgenstein's reaction was to reject the implication that there
was something intrinsically repulsive about sexuality. 'Why in the
world shouldn't they have regarded with awe and reverence that

act by which the human race is perpetuated? Not every religion has to have St Augustine's attitude to sex.'[40] Can we take this as evidence that Wittgenstein really changed his attitude to sex? It may well be so, but since we do not know of other similar episodes the evidence seems thin.

His love for Ben notwithstanding, Wittgenstein now found life in Cambridge increasingly intolerable. 'Everything about the place repels me', he noted in his diary. 'The stiffness, the artificiality, the self-satisfaction of the people. The university atmosphere nauseates me.'[41] More generally, he perceived the English civilization as 'disintegrating and putrefying'. He also felt much lonelier now. Francis, Ramsey, Keynes were all dead, while Drury, Malcolm and Rhees had left Cambridge. With Russell he had nothing to do any more, neither personally nor philosophically. Moore had suffered a stroke and his wife allowed him to talk to Wittgenstein for at the most one-and-a-half hours, which enraged Wittgenstein. Why should Moore not talk as much as he pleased? 'If he became very excited or tired and had a stroke and died – well, that would be a decent way to die: with his boots on.'[42] In addition, Wittgenstein was far from convinced that his teaching was doing any good. 'The only seed I am likely to sow is a certain jargon', he said in a lecture. And there was much truth to this, since there was a cult surrounding Wittgenstein in Cambridge, now considered the greatest living philosopher. As Gilbert Ryle described his visits to the Moral Sciences Club: 'veneration for Wittgenstein was so incontinent that mentions, for example my mentions, of other philosophers were greeted with jeers'.[43] This attitude was partly enforced by Wittgenstein himself, since he apparently not only prided himself with not having studied much history of philosophy, but also ridiculed those who had done so as 'academic philosophers'.

In the summer term of 1947 Wittgenstein decided to retire. He planned to leave England and live by himself. The summer he spent in Swansea, partly joined by Ben Richards, contemplating where to go next, Ireland or Norway. Eventually he chose Ireland. In September and October he visited his family in Vienna for the first time in eight years. Knowing about the post-war depression he dreaded seeing his native city again, and was indeed shocked by its devastation. The capital of the old empire in whose army he had once served was never to be the same again. What demoralized him in particular was the brutality of the Russians in their sector, where a lot of looting and raping was taking place. The Soviet troops had also vandalized the house he had built for Margarete. If Wittgenstein still had any illusions about the Soviets, he certainly lost them now. Back in Cambridge, he officially resigned his chair as from the end of the year, spent several more weeks at Trinity College preparing a typescript on the philosophy of psychology, and finally left for Dublin at the beginning of December. As he told Malcolm, 'I am in *no* way optimistic about my future but as soon as I had resigned I felt that it was the only natural thing to have done.'[44]

8

Nothing is Hidden: *Philosophical Investigations*

'The fox knows many things, but the hedgehog knows one big thing.' Isaiah Berlin once used this fragment by the Greek poet Archilocus to explain the deep divide between two kinds of writers and thinkers, indeed between two kinds of human beings. On the one hand, there are the hedgehogs – those who have a central vision, a coherent system, a universal principle, and relate everything to it. There are, on the other hand, the foxes – those whose thought moves on many levels, who are aware of the prodigious richness of phenomena and who do not try fitting it all into one unifying framework. Berlin classified Plato, Dante, Hegel, Dostoevsky as hedgehogs, Aristotle, Shakespeare, Goethe, Joyce as foxes, and Tolstoy as a cross of both.[1] But what about Wittgenstein? He, too, cannot be unequivocally placed into one or other category. By nature, he was a hedgehog, and his early work bears witness to this. For in the *Tractatus* he strived, like all great European metaphysicians, to encompass everything in a unifying system, everything from the foundations of logic to the nature of the world. But, as Peter Hacker has suggested, in his later work Wittgenstein transformed himself through great intellectual effort into a fox.[2]

Wittgenstein's early work was a paradigmatic example of system-building philosophy – his atomistic account of the essence of the proposition was the foundation upon which he built his theory of logic, language, ontology, mind and ethics. Everything was meant to hang together through one key assumption, namely that the essence of every elementary proposition is to describe a possible fact and to be independent of any other elementary proposition. Consequently, every statement had to be interpreted as a picture, even those that at face value did not seem to be picturing anything. The early philosophy was therefore analytical in a more literal sense: things are not as they seem to be; their hidden real essence is revealed to us when we step below the realm of appearances and analyse, that is, decompose the statement or a fact we are interested in into its actual constituents. True, the method employed for this, logical analysis, was new, but the aim, or rather the dream, of revealing the essence of things was as old as philosophy itself. It was the dream of establishing philosophy as metaphysics, a super-science discovering the most fundamental features of the world by means of the most rigorous method. And it was a dream that the early Wittgenstein thought had come true in his *Tractatus*.

But when, in 1929, he attempted to work out the programme of logical analysis announced in the book, he realized that his dream had been a chimera. His fundamental assumption proved to be wrong: there is no such thing as *the* essence of proposition, no such thing as *the* essence of language. And with it the entire logical, semantical and ontological edifice so meticulously developed in the *Tractatus* collapsed like a house of cards. By 1932 Wittgenstein had abandoned most of his old doctrines. But it was not only his specific doctrines that he came to reject – he demolished much of his earlier conception of philosophy itself. The main point that remained unchanged was his continuing belief that philosophy is not a science about the world, but consists in the *a priori* clarification of language. Among the major differences, by contrast, was his rejection of the metaphor of depth and the idea of a hidden essence, for 'Nothing is hidden' (*Philosophical Investigations* [PI] §435). All the philosopher is interested in lies in plain view. He need not dig down beneath the phenomena, but must stay on the ground level and draw a map of it. Geography replaces geology. This ground level consists of our language and the concepts expressed by it, including philosophically problematic ones like 'proposition', 'meaning', 'knowledge', 'ability', 'intention', 'number', etc. These basic notions constitute our conceptual framework, the grid through which we obtain knowledge about the world in both life and science. But since Wittgenstein now believes that none of these notions is more basic than the others, there can be no analysis in the older sense of the word, that is, there is no building of a system resting on one fundamental notion ('proposition' in the *Tractatus*), with all the others being reduced to, derived from or explained by it. All the philosopher has to do now instead is *describe*. He has to describe how the philosophically relevant concepts are related to each other, how 'proposition' and 'meaning', 'knowledge' and 'ability', etc., connect with one another. The new descriptive–connective method is really more like the drawing of a map. Wittgenstein employs the geographical metaphors himself in his Preface to the *Philosophical Investigations*, for he says that the nature of his investigation 'compels us to travel over a wide field of thought criss-cross in every direction. – The philosophical remarks in this book are, as it were, a number of sketches of landscapes which were made in the course of these long and involved journeyings.'[3] Later he writes: 'Our language can be seen as an ancient city: a maze of little streets and squares, of old and new houses, and of houses with additions from various periods; and this surrounded by a multitude of new boroughs with straight regular streets and uniform houses' (PI §18). This relates to another simile Wittgenstein gave his students in a lecture:

In teaching you philosophy I'm like a guide showing you how to find your way round London. I have to take you through the city from north to south, from east to west, from Euston to the embankment and from Piccadilly to the Marble Arch. After I

have taken you many journeys through the city, in all sorts
of directions, we shall have passed through any given street
a number of times – each time traversing the street as part of
a different journey. At the end of this you will know London;
you will be able to find your way about like a Londoner.[4]

Surveying our language in this way is not a self-contained
endeavour. Rather, we do it in order to solve philosophical problems
and puzzles. The later Wittgenstein is a truly linguistic philosopher, for he believes that most, if not all philosophical problems
arise through a misunderstanding of our language.

People say again and again that philosophy doesn't really
progress, that we are still occupied with the same philosophical
problems as were the Greeks. But the people who say this don't
understand why it had to be so. It is because our language has
remained the same and keeps seducing us into asking the same
questions. As long as there continues to be a verb 'to be' that
looks as if it functions in the same way as to 'eat' and 'to drink',
as long as we still have the adjectives 'identical', 'true', 'false',
'possible', as long as we continue to talk of a river of time, of an
expanse of space, etc. etc., people will keep stumbling over the
same puzzling difficulties and find themselves starting at something which no explanation seems capable of clearing up.[5]

Consequently these difficulties and problems can only be solved,
or rather dissolved, if we obtain a clear understanding of how our
language works. This attitude has two connected implications. First,
many philosophical questions are nonsensical, based on confusions
about how certain words work. Once we clarify these confusions
and we make the underlying nonsense patent, the questions do not
get answered, but simply dissolve. Philosophy is thus to a large
degree negative. As Wittgenstein himself put it while reflecting on

the nature of his thinking: 'I destroy, I destroy, I destroy'. Second, in philosophy we do not investigate the world in a trivial sense. We uncover or 'show' the metaphysical essence of the world, but only understand how our language works by giving what Wittgenstein calls a 'perspicuous representation of its grammar'. Since this involves giving an account of how individual expressions are employed in various everyday contexts in life and the sciences, knowledge about how and for which purpose words are used will involve knowledge about the world. But this is knowledge that we already have and that we simply recall or make explicit through the realization of affinities and differences in the familiar grammar of expressions. 'Learning in philosophy is *really* recollecting. We remember that we really did use words that way.' This is a far cry from traditional metaphysics and the metaphysics of the *Tractatus*.

What is philosophy? An enquiry into the essence of the world? . . . What we are in fact doing is to tidy up our notions, to make clear what *can* be said about the world. We are in a muddle about what can be said, and are trying to clear up that muddle. This activity of clearing up is philosophy.[6]

When philosophers use a word – 'knowledge', 'being', 'object', 'I', 'proposition', 'name' – and try to grasp the *essence* of the thing, one must always ask oneself: is the word ever actually used in this way in the language-game which is its original home? – What *we* do is to bring words back from their meta-physical to their everyday use [PI §116]. And this is what the solution of all philosophical difficulties looks like. Our answers, if they are correct, must be homely and trivial. But one must look at them in the proper spirit, and then that doesn't matter.[7]

This is a radically austere, disillusioning conception of philoso-phy with no precedent. If it is true, then the way philosophy has been done for the past 2,500 years is to a large extent misconceived. Wittgenstein was aware of these historical implications, despite his claim not to care about history. Thus, in a lecture in 1930 he described his philosophy as a new subject, a kink in the development of human thought. 'The nimbus of philosophy has been lost. For we now have a method of doing philosophy, and can speak of *skilful* philosophers. Compare the difference between alchemy and chemistry; chemistry has a method and we can speak of skilful chemists.' And around the same time he wrote in his diary: 'If my name survives, then only as the *terminus ad quem* of the great philosophy of the West. As the name of him who burnt the library of Alexandria.'[8] Unsurprisingly, this conception of philosophy has met with much resistance since Wittgenstein's death and it is at the moment to a large extent rejected by analytic philosophers. It is, contrary to the confidence in science characteristic of our time, a conception that greatly narrows the range of what we humans can know about the world through abstract thought. It resembles to some extent Immanuel Kant's critical philosophy, that is, the denial that pure reason is capable of answering the great metaphysical questions (about the existence of God, the immortality of the soul, the freedom of the will). Wittgenstein, however, is more radical than Kant, since he does not believe that our cognitive powers are too restricted to answer metaphysical questions, but that these very questions do not even make sense. Not even God could answer such questions. *Il faut cultiver notre jardin* – the modesty of Voltaire's Candide, which appealed so much to Kant, remains valid, but from Wittgenstein's point of view only because there is nothing else for philosophers outside the garden of grammar.

This view of philosophy is sketched in some fifteen pages of the *Philosophical Investigations* and applied in the rest of the book. Being the fruit of sixteen years of hard work the book is overly complex and cannot be summarized here in any detail.[9] It may suffice, however, to describe the character of the book and give a few examples of how philosophy is done in it. To begin with, it is short, just over 250 pages long in the English translation. From the ten thousands of remarks Wittgenstein made in his manuscripts since 1929 he selected only a tiny fragment and grouped them in 693 aphorism-like sections. We could thus view the *Investigations* as the tip of a massive iceberg. Three main areas are covered in the book: philosophy of language (meaning, understanding, following a rule, etc.), philosophy of mind (thinking, remembering, imagining, intending, etc.) and the already mentioned nature of philosophy. His extensive investigations into the philosophy of mathematics are only touched upon.

The style of the book is very different from that of the *Tractatus*. The prose is not so sibylline, but limpid and non-technical, with striking metaphors and analogies, thought experiments, invented language-games, rhetorical questions, soliloquies, etc. There are also several fragments of dialogue between a 'voice of error' and the 'voice of correctness' (which can often be construed as an exchange between young Ludwig and his present self), but it would be a mistake to view the entire book as a Socratic dialogue as some interpreters have done. For Wittgenstein was not a fan of the genre: 'Reading the Socratic dialogues one has the feeling; what a frightful waste of time! What's the point of these arguments that prove nothing and clarify nothing?'[10] Despite its clear style, the book has a dark side, a side that has fascinated and exasperated many readers. This is partly due to Wittgenstein's preference for 'the liberating word' and his aversion to redundancy. His remarks intimate more than they explicitly say, providing the reader with the seed of a thought, not with a spelled-out argument. Nevertheless, and despite his own liking of aphorists like Lichtenberg and Karl Kraus, it would not be accurate to regard the *Investigations* as a book of aphorisms, since it is a systematic and argumentative work in theoretical philosophy. But one often loses sight of its systematicity, because it is not always clear how the remarks connect and which topic, target or philosopher they specifically address. There is, in other words, no easily surveyable linear 'narrative', no immediate transparency of the author's intentions and convictions. This poses serious although not insurmountable challenges to the reader.

The *Investigations* deals with a very wide range of subjects, including the nature of the mind, intention, knowledge, thinking, etc. But the central theme of the book is the nature of language. It attempts to correct a hugely influential conception of language that has dominated European philosophy for centuries, indeed a conception that comes naturally to most humans when they begin to reflect on language. According to this conception, which was manifest in the *Tractatus* as well, the essence of language is to depict and describe reality. More precisely, this conception can be broken down into three main theses. First, the essential role of words is to name objects; the meaning of a word is the object it stands for. Second, language gets connected to the world via fundamental acts of naming; we point ostensively at an object and give the word '*A*' a meaning by saying 'This is *A*'. Third, the essential function of propositions is to describe how things are.

Wittgenstein argues in great detail against these theses and their ramifications, not only in the *Investigations*, but also in his writings on the philosophy of mathematics. First, he points out that names are not the fundamental type of word, contrary to what was explicitly assumed in the *Tractatus* or by Russell. Words do not fulfil only the function of naming or referring to objects. Their meaning is their use, roughly speaking (PI §43), and they can very well have a use without referring to anything. 'However', 'phlogiston' and 'gone with the wind' do not stand for any kind of object, despite having a well-established use. Russell's analysis of 'The present king of France is bald' (see chapter Two) arose out of desperation: since the subject-term 'the present king of France' does not refer to anything, he concluded that either it is meaningless, and thus the whole sentence is meaningless, or 'the present king of France' is a pseudo-referring expression and the real structure of the sentence is a totally different one, to be uncovered by logical analysis. But once we realize that 'the king of France' has a perfectly decent use whether or not it stands for anything, Russell's problem disappears and there is no need for his Theory of Descriptions.

Second, the act of naming is, although important, not fundamental. Indeed, it already presupposes mastery of a language.

> [T]he ostensive definition explains the use – the meaning – of the word when the overall role of the word in language is clear. Thus if I know that someone means to explain a colour-word to me the ostensive definition 'That is called "sepia"' will help me to understand the word. – And you can say this, so long as you do not forget that all sorts of problems attach to the words 'to know' or 'to be clear'. One has already to know (or be able to do) something in order to be capable of asking a thing's name [PI §30].

Third, Wittgenstein points out that the traditional conception of language dogmatically assumes that a certain type of propositions, which has some predominance in science, that is, the declarative subject-predicate-sentence (like 'Pluto is a planet'), represents the form of *all* sentences. But really, it is only one kind of proposition among many others, not the most fundamental one. For language does not have *one* function, but countless many. 'Language is an instrument. Its concepts are instruments' (PI §569). 'Look at the sentence as an instrument, and at its sense as its employment' (PI §421). And instruments have very different purposes. A prayer, a joke, a plea do not describe facts. When I say 'Buy me a diamond ring!' or ask 'How many fudges shall I eat today?' I am involved in very different language-games from that of describing, namely the language-game of ordering or that of asking questions respectively. These language-games are not less fundamental than those of describing, but equally fundamental, and it is a grave mistake to try to assimilate them to the language-game of describing. The declarative subject-predicate sentence is not the fundamental form of proposition.

> But how many kinds of sentence are there? Say assertion, question, and command? – There are *countless* kinds: countless different kinds of use of what we call 'symbols', 'words', 'sentences'. And this multiplicity is not something fixed, given once for all; but new types of language, new language-games, as we may say, come into existence, and others become obsolete and get forgotten . . . Here the term 'language-*game*' is meant to bring into prominence the fact that the *speaking* of language is part of an activity, or of a form of life [PI §23].

Since there is no fundamental kind of word and sentence, it is misleading to speak of the essence of language. The answer to the question 'What is language?' dissolves into an open-ended list of descriptions of various language-games. These language-games are more or less connected to each other, without having one unique feature in common. Wittgenstein compares the notion of language with that of a game. Can we give a precise definition of what a game is? What do all games have in common?

> Don't say: 'There *must* be something common, or they would not be called "games"' – but *look and see* whether there is any-thing common to all. – For if you look at them you will not see something that is common to *all*, but similarities, relationships, and a whole series of them at that. To repeat: don't think, but look! – Look for example at board-games, with their multifari-ous relationships. Now pass to card-games; here you find many correspondences with the first group, but many common fea-tures drop out, and others appear. When we pass next to ball-

games, much that is common is retained, but much is lost. –
Are they all 'amusing'? Compare chess with noughts and crosses.
Or is there always winning and losing, or competition between
players? Think of patience. In ball games there is winning and
losing; but when a child throws his ball at the wall and catches
it again, this feature has disappeared [PI §66].

Wittgenstein argues that the multifarious relationships between
these games are like the similarities between the members of a family. 'Game' is what Wittgenstein famously called a family resemblance concept, and its meaning cannot be captured by a *definition*.
Equally, 'language' is a family resemblance concept. Both concepts
lack sharp boundaries. But the vagueness of these concepts is only a
disadvantage if we think that the formal logic invented by Frege and
Russell *must* give us the standard of exactness or adequacy. There
is, however, no reason to believe this. Should we really say, as Frege
believed, that a word does not express a concept unless we can spec-
ify for any object in the universe whether it falls under the concept
or not? But that would not render only 'game' and 'language' use-
less, but also 'chair', 'terrorist', 'old' and 'bald'. If, during a photo-
shoot, the photographer circumscribes a certain area with his hand
and says to the model 'Stand roughly here', is he being unintelligible?
Would he do better if he used GPS technology? That would be
absurd and counterproductive. Vagueness is commonly part of the
usefulness of natural language. Indeed, even a concept such as that
of number is a family resemblance concept. From Wittgenstein's
point of view, Frege's monumental logicist project was based on the
failure to realize this.

> Why do we call something a 'number'? Well, perhaps because it
> has a – direct – relationship with several things that have hither-
> to been called number; and this can be said to give it an indirect
> relationship to other things we call the same name. And we

extend our concept of number as in spinning a thread we twist fibre on fibre. And the strength of the thread does not reside in the fact that some one fibre runs through its whole length, but in the overlapping of many fibres. But if someone wished to say: 'There is something common to all these constructions – namely the disjunction of all their common properties' – I should reply: Now you are only playing with words. One might as well say: 'Something runs through the whole thread – namely the continuous overlapping of those fibres' [PI §67].

Incidentally, we see here how Wittgenstein attempts to convince his interlocutor: by engaging him in a dialogue, giving him not only general arguments, but also many concrete examples, illuminating analogies, ironical replies. The *Investigations* is rich in passages of this kind.

Another example of the kind of arguments employed in the *Investigations* is Wittgenstein's discussion of the privacy of one's inner states. These inner states seem to be so private and unique that only I know what I am feeling. Others can only speculate. I myself may be mistaken about all my perceptions about the external world, but I am infallible as far as my inner world is concerned. This idea of subjective privacy comes not only as the most natural thing to most of us, but has been also very influential in European philosophy, especially in modern times. Given this privacy, I could even invent my own private language referring to my inner states which nobody else in the world could understand. Indeed, our ordinary language seems to be a kind of private language. For given the conception of language discussed above (i.e., the idea that a word has a meaning only insofar as it stands for some entity), one could argue that words have a meaning because of their link to internal mental states, emotions, pictures, ideas, etc. The meaning of a word is thus construed as something private, accessible only to the speaker himself – again a rather natural assumption of great historical influence. Witness for instance Locke in his *Essay Concerning Human Understanding* (1690): 'Words, in their primary or immediate signification, stand for nothing but the ideas in the mind of him that uses them . . . nor can anyone else apply them as marks, immediately, to anything else but the ideas that he himself hath'.[11] Humpty Dumpty puts it in *Alice in Wonderland* in a more straightforward manner: 'When *I* use a word, it means just what I choose it to mean – neither more nor less.'

Through powerful arguments Wittgenstein demonstrates not only that our ordinary language does not function in this way, but also that there cannot be any private language, since this is an incoherent idea (we shall skip his arguments here). Moreover, he attacks the idea of privacy itself and thus a pivotal assumption of European thought, showing how it rests on a misunderstanding of the function of psychological notions. Not only does he reject the idea that only I know what I am feeling, but he claims that really only other people can know what I am feeling. In other words, he actually rejects the claim that I know at all what I am feeling! By this, however, he does not mean that I am ignorant of my feelings either. Rather, it does not make *sense* to ascribe to me knowledge of my inner states. He demonstrates this claim by means of the descriptive method mentioned above. In other words, instead of taking it as basic or explaining it in terms of other concepts, Wittgenstein draws a map of the connections between knowledge and related concepts. For instance, he shows that knowledge is con-nected to the possibility of evidence, doubt, error, ignorance, etc. If these possibilities are excluded, so is knowledge. If they are included, so is knowledge. Take a case in which I have a headache and say 'I am in pain' while holding my head. It would surely make sense for *you* to look for evidence (my facial expression, for instance) whether I have a headache, but also to doubt this fact, err or be ignorant about it. Hence, it makes sense to ascribe to you the knowledge that I am in pain. But what about myself? Well, could I have a headache, but be ignorant about it and then find out about it through evidence offered to me? What could such evidence be? In what situation would it make sense to say of myself 'I may be in pain, but I doubt it'? And would it really be intelligible if I told my doctor in all seriousness 'Sorry, I was so sure a minute ago that I am in pain, but I have just discovered that I am mistaken'? None of this seems to work. The origin of the mistaken idea of privacy arises through misunderstanding the role of statements like 'I am in pain'. For they look like ordinary descriptions of a state of affairs, as in 'I am at Marble Arch'. It is, of course, possible to find out that or err that or doubt whether I am at Marble Arch and hence to know that I am at Marble Arch. But for all the similarity between 'I am at Marble Arch' and 'I am in pain', the latter sentence serves a very different function. 'Pain' is not the name of an inner, private state, and the sentence therefore is not a description of an inner, private state. Rather, 'I am in pain' is typically the *expression* or avowal of pain.

> A child has hurt himself and he cries; and then adults talk to him and teach him exclamations and, later, sentences. They teach the child new pain-behaviour. 'So you are saying that the word "pain" really means crying?' – On the contrary: the verbal expression of pain replaces crying and does not describe it [PI §244].

A related topic discussed by Wittgenstein is the concept of thinking. Again, it comes very naturally to us to conceive of thinking as a process happening inside our minds or brains, just as electronic processes are happening inside, let us say, a computer. This process inside us is supposed to be independent of any actual language we speak, for example, English or Swahili, and when we actually speak, we translate our inner thoughts into the public medium of language. As Thomas Hobbes put it in his *Leviathan* (1651): 'the general use of speech is to transfer our mental discourse into verbal, or the train of thoughts into a train of words'.[12] Indeed, this seems to explain how a child learns the meaning of 'thinking' or 'thought': it hears these words, looks inside itself and whatever it finds there is what 'thinking' refers to. This conception also allows for animals and computers to think, even though they might not have a language comparable to ours, if any. Again, Wittgenstein argues that this model of our cognitive life and the relation between thought and language resulting from it is not just simplistic but deeply mistaken. In conjuring up this model we are fixated on a certain way words receive their meaning, namely by pointing at something and then giving it a name, and we try to press the concept of thinking into this schema as well. But, Wittgenstein argues, this concept is neither learned nor used in this way, and unless we look carefully at the diverse and complex contexts in which the concept of thinking is actually used, we will at best achieve a caricature of this concept. 'It would be as if without knowing how to play chess, I were to try and make out what the word "mate" meant by close observation of the last move of some game of chess' (PI §316). We should be much more careful about the limited applications of the concept of thinking. 'We only say of a human being and what is like one that it thinks' (PI §360).

The chair is thinking to itself: . . . WHERE? In one of its parts? Or outside its body; in the air around it? Or not *anywhere* at all? But then what is the difference between this chair's saying something to itself and another one's doing so, next to it? – But then how is it with man: where does *he* say things to himself? How does it come about that this question seems senseless; and that no specification of a place is necessary except just that this man is saying something to himself? Whereas the question *where* the chair talks to itself seems to demand an answer. – The reason is: we want to know *how* the chair is supposed to be like a human being; whether, for instance, the head is at the top of the back and so on. What is it like to say something to oneself; what happens here? – How am I to explain it? Well, only as you might teach someone the meaning of the expression 'to say something to oneself'. And certainly we learn the meaning of that as children. – Only no one is going to say that the person who teaches it to us tells us 'what takes place' [PI §361].

If Wittgenstein is right, then when neuroscientists ask nowadays where our thinking is occurring, and then claim that it is occurring inside our brains, what they are actually doing is not treating a material object such as a chair like a human being, but a human being more like a chair! For the question as to where my thinking is taking place would otherwise not even arise. Is it really the case that when I am completing my tax return at my desk, my thinking is occurring in my brain, three inches behind my left eye? And that if I were to start jumping up and down on a trampoline, still thinking about my taxes, my thinking would also be bouncing up and down? Does this nonsense not show that we have a mistaken understanding of what thinking is? We should perhaps give up the idea that 'to think' and its cognates are employed to report or describe something that is going on inside me. How would the child that is learning the meaning of 'to think' even know what to look for inside itself? But is there not a 'stream of consciousness' going on inside me? Is this not thinking? Recording the 'stream of consciousness' (if it is at all clear what the phrase means), as James Joyce famously attempted in his *Ulysses*, has nothing to do with reporting what one thinks. When I say 'It is raining', I do report what I am thinking, namely that it is raining, but this is surely something that is happening *outside*, not in me, even if my thinking so is accompanied by all kinds of mental images or events. And there are other meanings of the phrase 'to think'. We must look at all these meanings in detail in order to understand the widely ramified concept of thinking.

Equally, the relation between thought and language is a very complex one. If the translation model were correct, then our thoughts must already be language-like, for how else could there be a *translation*? Thinking would be a kind of speaking, only to oneself, to one's soul (an influential idea in the history of philosophy). That would immediately open up the possibility of a person who constantly and unintentionally mistranslates their own thoughts – an absurdity. And would that 'language of thought' also have verb-like, noun-like and preposition-like elements? How did *they* receive their meaning? But if thoughts are not language-like, how are they like? What are they made of? Let us take the thought expressed by the following Cockney sentence: 'Iran's hard-line president on Saturday inaugurated a heavy-water produckshun plant, a facility th' Wess fears will be used t'develop a nucular bomb, as Tehran remained defiant ahaid of a UN daidline thet c'd lead t'sanckshuns.'[13] How could anybody even be *able* to entertain such a thought without speaking Cockney or at least some related language? Language is not just the clothing of thought, as Frege and the young Wittgenstein believed, but actually a presupposition for being able to have the articulate thoughts that we humans can have. The limits of thought are the limits of its possible expression. To put it in the extreme: there can be no thought without language. If correct, this claim is of major significance for any understanding of our mind, indeed for any anthropology. 'We say a dog is afraid his master will beat him; but not, he is afraid his master will beat him tomorrow. Why not?' (PI §650).

There are many other arguments and topics in the *Philosophical Investigations*. But we get a sense of how philosophy is done in this book and in general in Wittgenstein's later work. It is done for the purpose of preventing us from philosophical confusion by clarifying our language. This clarification, however, is not trivial in any way, but belongs to the most difficult intellectual activities.

Philosophy unravels the thoughts in our thinking; hence its result must be simple, but its activity as complicated as the knots it unravels . . . You ask why grammatical problems are so tough and seemingly ineradicable. – Because they are connected with the oldest thought habits, i.e. with the oldest images that are engraved into our language itself . . . Human beings are deeply embedded in philosophical, i.e. grammatical, confusions. And freeing them from these presupposes extricating them from the immensely diverse associations they are caught up in. One must, as it were, regroup their entire language . . . An entire mythology is laid down in our language.[14]

9

The Last Years, 1947–51

The last years in Wittgenstein's life were productive but marked by illness, loneliness and melancholia. He no longer had a home of his own, staying with friends or in hotels. In 1940 he had written in his diary 'I feel more dead than alive' and 'I feel my life has an ugly ending', and this was no less true in 1947 at the time of his resignation. As earlier in Norway, he now hoped to find solace through solitude in Ireland. With interruptions, he lived in Ireland from December 1947 to June 1949. The first few weeks he spent with Drury in Dublin, after which his friend arranged for him to stay with a family in a farmhouse in Red Cross, County Wicklow. At times he managed to write a good deal, mostly on the philosophy of psychology, experiencing such an outburst of inspiration that 'my ideas come so quickly that I feel as if my pen was being guided'. He prayed frequently, but his soul remained burdened. 'Feel unwell', he wrote in February 1948. 'Not physically, but mentally. Am frightened of the onset of insanity. God alone knows whether I am in danger.' Depression and the old guilt about Francis troubled him again.

> Don't let grief vex you! You should let it into your heart. Nor should you be afraid of madness. It comes to you perhaps as a friend and not as an enemy, and the only thing that is bad is your resistance . . . Think a great deal of the last time with Francis, of my odiousness towards him. I was at that time very unhappy; *but with a wicked heart*. I cannot see how I will ever in my life be freed from this guilt.[1]

Killary Bay, Connemara, Co. Galway, *c.* 1890–1900, a haunt of Wittgenstein's in Ireland.

Due to his nervous condition the farmhouse soon proved too noisy for him. Drury offered Wittgenstein his holiday cottage in Connemara, a district on the west coast of Ireland. The cottage, which faced the sea, gave him much needed rest. He stayed here until August and was looked after by Drury's servant, Thomas Mulkerrins. Wittgenstein went on long walks and was sometimes taken by Mulkerrins in a boat to the sea. He rarely socialized. His neighbouring family considered him so mad that they not only refused to have anything to do with him, but also forbade him to walk on their land for fear that he might scare their sheep.[2] But he had no concern with scaring sheep or other animals. On the contrary: he managed to tame some wild birds so well that they came to the window of his cottage and ate breadcrumbs out of his hand. Before he left Connemara, he even left money for Mulkerrins to feed them. Unfortunately, the birds' encounter with Wittgenstein eventually proved fatal: their tameness turned them into easy prey for the cats.[3]

After Connemara, Wittgenstein spent most of the time between October 1948 and June 1949 in Dublin. There he lodged in Ross's Hotel, content that he had a comfortable and quiet room, and was closer to Drury. Nevertheless, there were several other trips during this period. He visited Richards in Uxbridge a few times and also went to Cambridge. There he completed several manuscripts and visited Georg Henrik von Wright, a former student now successor to his chair in philosophy and fast becoming one of the most eminent philosophers of his generation. In September 1948 Wittgenstein travelled for three weeks to Vienna, where his sister Hermine was terminally ill. 'Mining is dying', he wrote in his diary in February 1949. 'A *great* loss for me and for everyone. *Greater* than I thought.' And a few weeks later: 'The roots on which my own life depend are being severed all around me. My soul is filled with pain. She had many and varied talents. Not exposed to the day, but hidden. As a person's qualities *should* be.'[4] He visited Vienna twice more, once in spring 1949 and finally from December 1949 to March 1950.

Wittgenstein's own health was failing. Having intestinal trouble, he went through a full check-up in Dublin in May 1949 and was diagnosed with an atypical form of anaemia. Nevertheless, Wittgenstein decided to undertake one final journey, this time to Ithaca in the United States. Norman Malcolm, who was teaching at Cornell University, had invited him on repeated occasions. To one of these invitations Wittgenstein jokingly replied that he would accept the invitation only if Malcolm would introduce him to Betty Hutton, Wittgenstein's favourite actress. Wittgenstein embarked on the *Queen Mary* to New York in July, travelling third class. Insisting, to no avail, that Malcolm should not pick him up on arrival, Wittgenstein wrote to his friend: 'Maybe, like in the films, I'll find a beautiful girl whom I meet on the boat & who will help me.' Wittgenstein stayed with the Malcolms for three months. Overall, he enjoyed his stay. He wrote to Rhees in Swansea:

Wittgenstein with his Finnish philosopher friend Georg Henrik von Wright.

There are some nice walks here though nothing compared with the [G]ower coast. Nature here doesn't look as *natural* as in Wales. The only thing I really enjoy here is the *engineering*; that's superb. I like to see American machines. The people I've met were often very nice but mostly, though not always, very foreign to me.[5]

Although he himself felt that he was no longer capable of doing philosophy, the philosophers he met at Cornell, for example Max Black, John Nelson and Oets Bouwsma, received a different impression. He gave talks and attended, or rather dominated, numerous seminars and discussions, dazzling everybody with his personality. As Nelson remembers, an encounter with Wittgenstein was

probably the most philosophically strenuous two hours I have ever spent. Under the relentless probing and pushing of his inquiry my head felt almost as if it were ready to burst . . . There was no quarter given – no sliding off the topic when it became difficult. I was absolutely exhausted when we concluded the discussion.[6]

Wittgenstein was, according to Nelson, a mysterious and awesome name at Cornell in 1949. When Max Black addressed Wittgenstein during a lecture with 'I wonder if you would be so kind, Professor Wittgenstein', a gasp went up from the audience. It was as if Black had said 'I wonder whether you would be so kind, Plato'.[7] Wittgenstein's longest discussions were with Malcolm and with Bouwsma, a philosopher influenced by Moore.

With Malcolm he discussed problems relating to epistemology, especially knowledge and scepticism, a topic he had not touched upon since the *Tractatus*. Wittgenstein's subsequent notes on these themes, published as *On Certainty* in 1969, preoccupied him until his death. They are numerous and original, but he never brought them to a polished form. His answer to the traditional problem of scepticism (How do I know that the world exists? How do I know that this tree really exists?) was to some extent similar to what he had stated in the *Tractatus*: 'Scepticism is *not* irrefutable, but obviously nonsensical, when it tries to raise doubts where no question can be asked' (*Tractatus* 6.51). Wittgenstein now gave not only more detailed arguments supporting this thesis, but proposed a solution to the problem of scepticism more in line with his later philosophy. He argued that the sceptic does not genuinely question or doubt our ordinary knowledge and experience, but actually fails to pose any sensible question at all. For the language-game of doubting is only learned by the child against an undoubted background, and thus presupposes the latter. You can only doubt something if you presuppose something else as unquestionable. If you question everything at once, you are sawing off the branch on which you are sitting and which allows you to doubt something. The term 'doubt', as employed by the sceptic, is thus a meaningless term, since it is taken out of its customary context. This is missed both by the sceptic and by his opponent, for example, a Cartesian philosopher, who first takes the sceptic's radical doubt seriously and then looks for true propositions, known with absolute certainty, to counter the radical doubt. G. E. Moore, for instance, argued that common-sense propositions like 'This is a hand' (while raising his hand), 'That's a tree' (while standing in front of one) or 'The world has existed for many years' are such absolutely certain propositions which we can employ against the sceptic. Wittgenstein's answer is that in philosophical contexts these propositions do not express any knowledge at all, but belong to our conceptual frame-work, our world picture. Rejecting them is not like rejecting 'Sushi is increasingly popular in London' or 'Iran has peaceful intentions', rather it is like upsetting the entire world picture and thus the frame-work within which the language-games of knowing and doubting make sense at all. 'If Moore were to pronounce the opposite of those propositions which he declares certain, we should not just not share his opinion: we should regard him as demented.'[8] In short, what both the sceptic and his Cartesian opponent really achieve is not radical doubt and absolute knowledge respectively, but the dismissal of rationality itself – not an insignificant insight in an age of far-reaching conspiracy theories and historical revisionisms that have a lot in common with the sceptic's attitude to knowledge.

Wittgenstein's discussions with Bouwsma touched on more general issues as well. For instance, he stressed that there are some similarities between his philosophy and psychoanalysis, in both positive and negative respects. He thought that his teachings, like Freud's, had done more harm than good, seducing students to believe in an all-solving 'formula'. Wittgenstein also expressed his dislike of Plato's dialogues to Bouwsma:

The Socratic method! The arguments were bad, the pretence of discussion too obvious, the Socratic irony distasteful – why can't a man be forthright and say what's on his mind? As for the Socratic method . . . it simply isn't there. The interlocutors are ninnies, never have any arguments of their own, say 'Yes' and 'No' as Socrates pleases they should. They are a stupid lot.[9]

One evening Bouwsma took Wittgenstein to a hill overlooking the town. Viewing the panorama Wittgenstein said something characteristic of the unfathomable side of his personality: 'If I had planned it, I should not have made the sun at all. See! How beautiful! The sun is too bright and too hot . . . And if there were only the moon there would be no reading and writing.'[10]

While in Ithaca, Wittgenstein fell ill and had to undergo examination in a hospital. Suspecting he might have cancer, he feared that he would have to undergo surgery and not be able to return to Europe. He said to Malcolm in frenzy: 'I don't want to die in America. I am a European – I want to die in Europe . . . What a fool I was to come.'[11] Luckily, the examination turned out well and Wittgenstein was able to return safely to England at the end of October. After a brief stay in London he visited von Wright in Cambridge. The plan was to return to Ross's Hotel in Dublin. But while in Cambridge he fell sick again and was once more examined, this time by Dr Edward Bevan, the family doctor of the von Wrights and an acquaintance of Drury. Soon after this examination Wittgenstein wrote to Malcolm:

Dear Norman, Thanks for your letter! The doctors have now made their diagnosis. I have cancer of the prostate. But this sounds, in a way, much worse than it is, for there is a drug (actually some hormones) which can, as I'm told, alleviate the symptoms of the disease, so that I can live on for years. The doctor even tells me that I may be able to work again, but I can't imagine that. I was in no way shocked when I heard I had cancer, but I *was* when I heard that one could do something about it, because I had *no* wish to live on. But I cou[l]dn't have my wish. I am treated with great kindness by every one & I have an

immensely kind doctor who isn't a fool either. I think of you &
[your wife] often with gratitude . . . Affectionately, Ludwig[12]

He was prescribed oestrogen, which was supposed to prolong his
life for several years, and some time later received x-ray treatment.
As he commented to Rhees, 'Another year of this half-life would
have been ample.'[13] Initially, Wittgenstein kept his illness a secret
from most people around him, including his family. He flew to
Vienna for Christmas to be with Hermine, who died in February
1950, and returned to England a month later. For the remaining
year of his life he stayed with various friends, while continuing,
with interruptions, either to revise his existing manuscripts or even,
despite his physical condition, to work on new material, especially
on epistemology and colours. From April to October 1950 he lodged
in Oxford, at 27 St John Street, with Elizabeth Anscombe, his
former pupil and probably the most eminent female philosopher
of the twentieth century. It was here that he re-read Shakespeare's
works, for which he had a restrained admiration.

> [I]f Shakespeare is great, his greatness is displayed only in the
> whole *corpus* of his plays, which create their *own* language and
> world. In other words he is completely unrealistic. (Like a
> dream.) . . . I could only stare in wonder at Shakespeare, never
> do anything with him . . . 'Beethoven's great heart' – nobody
> could speak of 'Shakespeare's great heart' . . . People stare at
> him in wonderment, almost as a spectacular natural phenome-
> non. They do not have the feeling that this brings them into
> contact with a great *human being*. Rather with a phenomenon.[14]

Wittgenstein befriended another lodger in Anscombe's house,
Barry Pink, who, like Anscombe and other friends of Wittgenstein,
was a convert to Catholicism. During one of their intimate conversations, Pink asked Wittgenstein whether his philosophy had anything

Wittgenstein's last entry in his diary, two days before his death.

to do with his homosexuality. Such questions have been asked after Wittgenstein's death. Colin Wilson, for instance, has suggested that young Wittgenstein's inability to resist homosexual tendencies produced in him 'the craving for certainty that lead him to create the philosophical system of the *Tractatus*'.[15] This is of course plain nonsense. The theory of logic proposed in Wittgenstein's early book or his complex elucidations of natural language and the foundations of mathematics given in his later work have as much to do with his sexuality as Kant's transcendental idealism with his (largely) chaste life or Einstein's theory of relativity with his various extra-marital affairs. We would certainly be able to understand, discuss, approve or refute the works of all these thinkers even if we swapped their 'sexual identities' (Wittgenstein as an unfaithful husband, Kant a troubled homosexual and Einstein as a chaste bachelor). No wonder that Wittgenstein dismissed Pink's question angrily with a 'Certainly not!'[16]

While in Oxford Wittgenstein felt that his life was coming to an end, and he asked Anscombe to put him in touch with a Catholic priest, Father Conrad Pepler. As the latter remembers, Wittgenstein wanted to talk to a priest and did not wish to discuss philosophical problems. He knew he was very ill and wanted to talk about God, I think with a view to coming back fully to his religion, but in fact we had, I think, only two conversations on God and the soul on rather general terms.[17]

The possibility that Wittgenstein might have wanted to embrace the Catholic faith, in which he had been baptized, might be doubted given his avowed inability to believe that its doctrines were literally true. But it is not impossible. The episode shows that in the last months of his life Wittgenstein was perhaps driven by a will to believe, representative of his lifelong concern with religious matters. It also shows that he took such matters to be sharply distinguished from philosophy.

In October 1950 Wittgenstein undertook his last long journey, travelling with Ben Richards to Norway for a month. They stayed in his old hut and, when Richards fell ill, with Wittgenstein's old host, Anna Rebni. Wittgenstein greatly enjoyed this stay and decided to come back soon on his own. However, this and similar plans for a solitary existence were thwarted when his health began to decline rapidly in January 1951. After examination it was understood that he had only a few months to live and medication terminated. He needed constant care now, but was horrified at the prospect of having to die in a hospital. In these circumstances Dr Bevan came forward with a remarkably generous offer: he invited Wittgenstein to spend his last days in Bevan's house in Cambridge – without any payment. Wittgenstein accepted and moved into his last home in February. He was looked after by Bevan's wife, who not only prepared his baths and provided him with food and books, but also bought him his much beloved *Street & Smith's Detective Story Magazine*[18] and accompanied him every evening to the local pub, where they had friendly, unpretentious chats. Remarkably, in his two months with the Bevans Wittgenstein experienced one last outburst of creativity,

Wittgenstein's grave in Cambridge.

composing the second half of the remarks of *On Certainty*, many of which betray the best features of his writing: clarity and incisiveness. In an unusually self-ironical passage he even poked fun at himself: 'I do philosophy now like an old woman who is always mislaying something and having to look for it again; now her spectacles, now her keys'.[19] His last entry in his last diary, a reflection on believing, dreaming and losing one's consciousness, occurred a day after his 62nd birthday and two days before his death. He died on the morning of 29 April 1951. Before he lost consciousness he told Mrs Bevan: 'Tell them I've had a wonderful life'. On the decision of his Catholic friends he was given a Catholic burial at St Giles's Church, Cambridge.

10

The Aftermath

Wittgenstein left the task of editing and publishing his gigantic *Nachlass*, that is, his notebooks, manuscripts and typescripts amounting to 20,000 pages, to his literary executors, Anscombe, Rhees and von Wright. After his death the publication of his works was an urgent matter, since his later ideas were known only to a small circle of devotees and otherwise only from hearsay. In 1953 *Philosophical Investigations* was finally published, in a bilingual version, with the English translation by Anscombe. Many reviewers soon praised the book. Peter Strawson, for instance, starts his review of the *Investigations*, one of the very first, with the following lines:

> This book is a treatment, by a philosopher of genius, of a number of intricate problems, intricately connected. It also presents in itself an intricate problem: that of seeing clearly what the author's views are on the topics he discusses, and how these views are connected.[1]

Over the next decades many more volumes of his writings, lectures and conversations came out. Finally in 2001 his entire *Nachlass*, including facsimiles of all his manuscripts, was published in a CD-ROM version.

Up to the 1970s Wittgenstein's influence upon the development of philosophy was decisive, especially in Oxford, a stronghold of post-war analytic philosophy, where some of his pupils and collaborators, such as Anscombe, Toulmin and Waismann, taught side by side with a generation of younger thinkers influenced by or sympathetic to Wittgenstein's works. In Cambridge he was succeeded in his chair first by von Wright, then by John Wisdom and finally by Anscombe. Wittgenstein's influence spread from Britain to the rest of the English-speaking world. In the US Norman Malcolm and Max Black transformed the philosophy faculty at Cornell into one of the leading departments in the country. Erik Stenius, Georg Henrik von Wright and Jaakko Hintikka ensured the transmission of his ideas in Scandinavia. On the Continent interest in his work arose more slowly, partly due to lack of interest in analytic philosophy and the influence of other philosophers, such as Husserl and Heidegger. His work was also well received in Asia, particularly in Japan and more recently in China. At the time of his greatest influence in the Anglo-Saxon world many branches of philosophy were affected by his work, including some about which he had written little to nothing, such as the philosophy of the social sciences and moral, legal and political philosophy. His strongest impact, however, affected the core disciplines of theoretical philosophy, especially philosophy of logic, language and mind (not, however, philosophy of mathematics). His conception of philosophy as a non-scientific linguistic investigation of our conceptual framework was also influential. In those days there was an assumption among his supporters that armed with Wittgenstein's method one could finally get down to business and solve the great problems of philosophy. As Anthony Kenny has put it in retrospect, they 'had imagined that once his philosophical ideas had been absorbed, thinkers in various disciplines would begin to apply them, with beneficial effect, to work in their own field'.[2]

Ironically, however, just when Wittgenstein's oeuvre became more and more accessible, the influence of his ideas declined among academic philosophers. The most important reason for this is the fact that his ideas were submerged by the rise of new metaphysics and scientifically inspired philosophy, which emanated particularly strongly from the US, where philosophers such as Willard van Orman Quine, Donald Davidson, David Lewis, Saul Aaron Kripke and Noam Chomsky were active. Equally important for the development of Anglo-American philosophy was the emergence of new scientific disciplines such as computer science, molecular and evolutionary biology, neuroscience and cognitive psychology. It is likely that Wittgenstein would have perceived such scientification of philosophy as symptomatic of the malaise of modernity. He once said to Drury: 'My type of thinking is not wanted in this present age; I have to swim so strongly against the tide. Perhaps in a hundred years people will really want what I am writing.'[3] The future will tell. To be sure, the *Tractatus* and the *Investigations* are today regarded as classics. In a 1998 poll among professional philosophers, Wittgenstein was ranked fifth among the all-time greats, after Aristotle, Plato, Kant and Nietzsche, and ahead of Hume and Descartes. And another poll, conducted in 2000, resulted in the *Philosophical Investigations* being voted as the most important philosophical work of the twentieth century, with the *Tractatus* ranking as fourth. But nominal popularity does not mean philosophical dominance. On the contrary: a glance at the leading philosophy journals will show that his philosophy, particularly his later philosophy, is today being marginalized.

In the light of the 10,000 books and articles published on Wittgenstein by the end of the twentieth century such claims may seem implausible. After all, Wittgenstein's works need to be edited and interpreted just as much as, for instance, Aristotle's or Kant's works. But the 'Wittgenstein industry' goes beyond what is necessary and almost obscures access to Wittgenstein's thought by producing countless competing interpretations, philological debates, new 'readings', introductions, textbooks for students, collections of papers, conference proceedings, dissertations, etc. This industry produces with remarkable regularity titles such as *The New Wittgenstein*,

Wittgenstein's Poker, Wittgenstein's Ladder, The Third Wittgenstein,
Wittgenstein in 90 Minutes, Wittgenstein Flies a Kite, etc. Looking at
this scholastic output, one sometimes gets the impression that it is
diametrically opposed to what Wittgenstein hoped to achieve. For
he surely did not want to create a branch of specialists writing *about*
him and his works, but to revolutionize philosophy itself.

However, the fact that Wittgenstein scholarship is flourishing,
while Wittgensteinian philosophy has withered, may also be due
to the problem 'of seeing clearly what the author's views are', as
Strawson put it in the review mentioned above. For a major difficulty
with Wittgenstein's work lies in the unusual character of his writings, which invite conflicting readings and endless controversies. We
may wonder whether Wittgenstein's attitude to philosophical prose,
the intrusion of aesthetic criteria into his discourse, has not been
detrimental to the reception of his work. It is noteworthy that he
was himself more critical of his style than some of his contemporary
supporters, as a sequence of remarks from the 1940s demonstrates.
In 1941 he wrote in his diary 'My style is like bad musical composition', while in 1945 he admitted in the Preface to the *Philosophical
Investigations* that the best that he could write would never be more
than philosophical remarks. In 1948 he noted down a striking simile:

> Raisins may be the best part of a cake; but a bag of raisins is not
> better than a cake; & someone who is in a position to give us a
> bag full of raisins still cannot bake a cake with them, let alone
> do something better. I am thinking of Kraus & his aphorisms,
> but of myself too & my philosophical remarks. A cake is not as
> it were: thinned out raisins.[4]

Wittgenstein's attempt to combine philosophical arguments with
the perfect expression, 'the liberating word', is not unique in modern
philosophy. We find it in various forms in Continental philosophers,
for instance in Hegel, Hölderlin or Nietzsche, and more expressly

The opening page from Elizabeth Lutyens's piece of 1952–3 for unaccompanied voices, *Motet Excerpta Tractati Logico-Philosophici* (known as the 'Wittgenstein Motet').

so in twentieth-century figures like Heidegger, Benjamin, Adorno and Derrida, thinkers who, to various degrees and for different rationales, expressly chose particular styles of writing. The heightened self-awareness of the act of writing is actually a very modern trait, to be found not only in philosophy, but even more so in literature, if we think only of writers such as James Joyce, Marcel Proust or André Gide. Wittgenstein fits well in this modernist current, although his case is unique, since in important respects he belongs to analytic philosophy, a philosophical current that has greater affinities to logic, mathematics and natural science than to Continental philosophy and literature.[5] The Janus-faced trait of his *oeuvre*, which results from his affinities to two different intellectual currents, makes it fascinating, but also poses great difficulties to its interpretation, and this may partly explain the 'industry' surrounding his work.

So much for Wittgenstein's standing within academic philosophy at present. Like Freud's, however, Wittgenstein's impact reached far beyond academia. Already a legend in his own lifetime, in the age of pop culture Wittgenstein has become almost a pop star, 'the thinking man's hero', as a television programme put it. A motet based on the *Tractatus* was composed by Elizabeth Lutyens and a *Tractatus Suite* by M. A. Numminem. Eduardo Paolozzi etched a set of prints entitled 'Wittgenstein in New York', while Derek Jarman directed the successful film *Wittgenstein*, based on a script by Terry Eagleton. Several novels inspired by his life were published, such as *Wittgenstein's Nephew* by the congenial Austrian writer Thomas Bernard, *Malina* by the equally congenial Austrian poet Ingeborg Bachmann (who also lectured on Wittgenstein and Heidegger) and *The World as I Found It* by Bruce Duffy. Moreover, the sibylline remarks of the *Tractatus*, especially those on ethics, and the numerous striking aphorisms from his later period have appealed to a wide audience and are often quoted. Alas, they are rarely understood, given that they are mostly not self-sufficient aphorisms, but the rhetorical tips of a vast iceberg of systematic thought. More recently, Wittgenstein has been also portrayed as a postmodernist, a relativist, a poet (or even as a Pyrrhonist, Zen-Buddhist or rabbinical thinker). These are strange interpretations of a man who towards the end of his life said that his chief contribution had been in the philosophy of mathematics:[6] a man who in his youth vowed that he did not intend 'to prove this and that, but to find out how things really are'[7] and who later said: 'I know my method is right. My father was a businessman, and I am a business man: I want my philosophy to be businesslike, to get something done, to get something settled.'[8] All this does not square well with postmodernist wariness, insecurity and quietism.

Nevertheless, there is something understandable about the popular fascination with Wittgenstein, the alluring archetype of a tormented thinker.

From time to time in our culture, literary and artistic figures become objects of veneration in circles far wider than the reach of their works. Their lives are held to be of deeper significance than the mere fascination of their biography. Their travails and their intellectual and spiritual strivings are inchoately sensed to incorporate and to represent the deepest tensions and conflicts within the culture of their times. So, perhaps, it has been with Ludwig Wittgenstein.[9]

This, then, may explain our fascination with Wittgenstein: that despite his intellectual achievements, he never found his *Sitz im Leben*, his place in life – like modern man. He strove to be perfect, but his life remained a fragment, rich in triumphs, contradictions and failings. It was in this sense that his life was beautiful, or rather paradigmatic. 'After somebody has died we see his life in a conciliatory light. His life looks well-rounded through a haze. For *him* it was not well-rounded however, but jagged & incomplete. For him there was no reconciliation; his life is naked & wretched.'[10]

Karl Johnson in the title role of Derek Jarman's 1983 film *Wittgenstein*, shown in a cage – with a parrot in another cage.

References

1 Family and Early Years, 1889–1911

1 For more, see E. Timms, *Karl Kraus: Apocalyptic Satirist. Culture and Catastrophe in Habsburg Vienna* (New Haven, CT, and London, 1986), pp. 3–39.

2 U. Weinzierl, 'Der Fluch des Hauses Wittgenstein', *Die Welt* (5 July 2003).

3 R. Monk, *Ludwig Wittgenstein: The Duty of Genius* (London, 1990), p. 13. This is based on what Wittgenstein had told Rush Rhees, who in turn told it to Ray Monk.

4 B. McGuinness, *Young Ludwig: Wittgenstein's Life, 1889–1921* (Oxford, 2005), p. 26.

5 M. Nedo and M. Ranchetti, *Wittgenstein: Sein Leben in Bildern und Texten* (Frankfurt, 1983), p. 54.

6 M. Drury, 'Conversations with Wittgenstein', in *Ludwig Wittgenstein: Personal Recollections*, ed. R. Rhees (Oxford, 1981), p. 27.

7 K. Cornish, *The Jew of Linz* (London, 1998).

8 Monk, *Ludwig Wittgenstein*, p. 15.

9 See B. Hamann, *Hitler's Vienna: A Dictator's Apprenticeship* (Oxford, 1999).

10 Rhees, *Ludwig Wittgenstein*, p. 2.

11 Monk, *Ludwig Wittgenstein*, p. 16.

12 McGuinness, *Young Ludwig*, pp. 47–8.

13 Monk, *Ludwig Wittgenstein*, p. 498.

14 Ibid., p. 78.

15 Ibid., p. 23.

16 Ibid., pp. 23ff.

17 Drury, 'Conversations with Wittgenstein', in Rhees, *Ludwig Wittgenstein*, p. 106.

18 O. Weininger, *Sex and Character* (London, 1906), p. 147.

19 McGuinness, *Young Ludwig*, p. 54.

2 Cambridge, Norway and Philosophy, 1911–14

1 H. R. Hertz, *The Principles of Mechanics* (London, 1899), pp. 7–8.

2 B. McGuinness, *Young Ludwig: Wittgenstein's Life, 1889–1921* (Oxford, 2005), pp. 73–4.

3 There are recent attempts to revive Frege's logicism, most notably by George Boolos and Crispin Wright.

4 Since Wittgenstein's letter has not survived, we do not know what his attempted solution was.

5 E. Anscombe and P. Geach, *Three Philosophers* (Oxford, 1967), p. 130.

6 For a possible interpretation of this matter, see McGuinness, *Young Ludwig*, pp. 89–92.

7 Letter to Lady Ottoline Morrell, 16 March 1912; R. Monk, *Ludwig Wittgenstein: The Duty of Genius* (London, 1990), p. 43.

8 B. Russell, *Autobiography* (London, 2000), p. 329.

9 Monk, *Ludwig Wittgenstein*, p. 48.

10 See McGuinness, *Young Ludwig*, pp. 127–8.

11 David Pinsent, Diary, 30 May 1912.

12 Ibid., 25 August 1913.

13 Ibid., 12 July 1912.

14 Letter to Lady Ottoline Morrell, 5 September 1912.

15 Pinsent, Diary, 5 September 1912.

16 See McGuinness, *Young Ludwig*, pp. 53, 122–3.

17 Ibid., p. 123.

18 Monk, *Ludwig Wittgenstein*, p. 63.

19 Letter to Lady Ottoline Morrell, 13 October 1912; Monk, *Ludwig Wittgenstein*, p. 53.

20 Letter to Lady Ottoline Morrell, 9 November 1912; Monk, *Ludwig Wittgenstein*, p. 65.

21 Letter to Lady Ottoline Morrell, 27 May 1913; Monk, *Ludwig Wittgenstein*, pp. 81–2.

22 Letter to Lady Ottoline Morrell, 1916; Monk, *Ludwig Wittgenstein*, pp. 80–81.

23 L. Wittgenstein, *Philosophical Occasions* (Indianapolis, IN, 1993), pp. 2–3.

24 For Wittgenstein's relation to Norway, see K. S. Johannessen, R. Larsen and K. O. Åmås, *Wittgenstein and Norway* (Oslo, 1994).

25 Monk, *Ludwig Wittgenstein*, p. 86.

26 L. Wittgenstein, *Cambridge Letters*, ed. B. McGuiness and G. H. von Wright (Oxford, 1995).

27 Letter to Lucy Mary Donnelly, 19 October 1913; McGuinness, *Young Ludwig*, p. 184.

28 Goodstein, in *Ludwig Wittgenstein: Philosophy and Language*, ed. A. Ambrose and M. Lazerowitz (London, 1972), pp. 271–2.

29 L. Wittgenstein, *Culture and Value* (Oxford, 1980), p. 87e.

30 Letter to Russell, presumably December 1913, in Wittgenstein, *Cambridge Letters*.

31 Letter to Russell, January 1914, ibid.

32 Letter to Russell, February 1914, ibid.

33 Letter to Moore, 7 May 1914, ibid.

34 Constantin Noica (1909–1987), Romanian philosopher. See G. Liiceanu, *The Paltinis Diary* (Budapest, 2000).

35 Monk, *Ludwig Wittgenstein*, p. 107.

36 Letter to Ficker, 13 February 1915, ibid., p. 110.

37 McGuinness, *Young Ludwig*, p. 209.

38 A. Sarnitz, *Adolf Loos* (London, 2003).

3 In the Trenches, 1914–18

1 MS 101, 25 October 1914. All manuscript references refer to Wittgenstein's *Nachlass* (Bergen and Oxford, 2000).

2 MS 101, 18 August 1914.

3 MS 101, 13 September 1914.

4 MS 102, 8 December 1914.

5 B. McGuinness, *Young Ludwig: Wittgenstein's Life, 1889–1921* (Oxford, 2005), p. 238.

6 MS 103, 4 May 1916.

7 MS 103, 29 March 1916.

8 MS 103, 30 April 1916.

9 MS 103, 30 March 1916.

10 MS 103, 11 June 1916.

11 MS 103, 6 July 1916.

12 MS 103, 30 July 1916.

13 MS 103, 28 August 1916.

14 McGuinness, *Young Ludwig*, p. 242.

15 Ibid., p. 252.

16 MS 103, 7 October 1916. *Sub specie aeternitatis* means 'under the aspect of eternity'.

17 B. McGuinness, *Approaches to Wittgenstein: Collected Papers* (London, 2002), p. 34.

18 Ibid., pp. 34–5.

19 McGuinness, *Young Ludwig*, p. 263.

20 Ibid., p. 264.

21 MS 102, 16 March 1915.

4 Logic and Mysticism: The *Tractatus*

1 See, e.g., M. Perloff, *Wittgenstein's Ladder: Poetic Language and the Strangeness of the Ordinary* (Chicago, IL, 1996); D. Rozema, '*Tractatus Logico-Philosophicus*: A "Poem" by Ludwig Wittgenstein', *Journal of the History of Ideas*, LXIII/2 (2002).

2 See T. Eagleton, 'Introduction to Wittgenstein', in *Wittgenstein: The Terry Eagleton Script; The Derek Jarman Film* (Worcester, MA, 1993), p. 5.

3 L. Wittgenstein, *The Big Typescript: TS 213* (Oxford, 2005), p. 302e.

4 L. Wittgenstein, *Culture and Value* (Oxford, 1980), p. 39e.

5 Ibid., p. 24e.

6 R. Rhees, ed., *Recollections of Wittgenstein* (Oxford, 1984), p. 159.

7 Letter to Lady Ottoline Morrell, 27 May 1912; R. Monk, *Ludwig Wittgenstein: The Duty of Genius* (London, 1990), p. 54.

8 Monk, *Ludwig Wittgenstein*, p. 178.

9 Letter to Russell, 19 August 1919; L. Wittgenstein, *Cambridge Letters*, ed. B. McGuiness and G. H. von Wright (Oxford, 1995).

5 The Wilderness Years, 1918–29

1 Letter to von Ficker, October 1919; B. McGuinness, *Young Ludwig: Wittgenstein's Life, 1889–1921* (Oxford, 2005), p. 287.

2 McGuinness, *Young Ludwig*.

3 Ibid.

4 Ibid., p. 274.

5 Ibid., p. 280.

6 Letter to Russell, 6 October 1919; L. Wittgenstein, *Cambridge Letters*, ed. B. McGuiness and G. H. von Wright (Oxford, 1995).

7 Letter to Engelmann, 30 May 1920; P. Engelmann, *Letters from Ludwig Wittgenstein with a Memoir* (Oxford, 1967).

8 W. W. Bartley III has made the allegation that Wittgenstein felt so low because he could not stay away from an area in the city's park frequented by homosexual young men. Bartley does not produce any evidence for this allegation. See Bartley, *Wittgenstein* (La Salle, IL, 1986), and, for a critical discussion, R. Monk, *Ludwig Wittgenstein: The Duty of Genius* (London, 1990), pp. 581ff.

9 Letter to Russell, 6 August 1920; Wittgenstein, *Cambridge Letters*.

10 Letter to Russell, 20 September 1920; Wittgenstein, *Cambridge Letters*.

11 Monk, *Ludwig Wittgenstein*, p. 194.

12 Ibid., p. 196.

13 Ibid., pp. 195–6.

14 Letter to Engelmann, 2 January 1921; Engelmann, *Letters*.

15 See Monk, *Ludwig Wittgenstein*, p. 181.

16 B. Russell, *Autobiography* (London, 2000), p. 332.

17 R. Rhees, ed., *Ludwig Wittgenstein: Personal Recollections* (Oxford, 1981), pp. 127–8.

18 Ramsey to his mother, 20 September 1923; quoted in Monk, *Ludwig Wittgenstein*, p. 216.

19 See Monk, *Ludwig Wittgenstein*, p. 234.

20 See, e.g., E. C. Hargrove, 'Wittgenstein, Bartley, and the Glöckel School Reform', *Journal of the History of Philosophy*, XVIII (1980), p. 461. See also Bartley, *Wittgenstein*.

21 Engelmann, *Letters*, pp. 114–15.

22 Like other original manuscripts and editions, the dictionary is now a much valued item among collectors. In 2005 the proofs of the dictionary

sold for £75,000.

23 See J. Hintikka, *On Wittgenstein* (Belmont, CA, 2000).

24 Monk, *Ludwig Wittgenstein*, p. 235.

25 Funnily enough, companies now sell door handles *à la* Wittgenstein.

26 Monk, *Ludwig Wittgenstein*, p. 236.

27 See B. Leitner, *The Wittgenstein House* (New York, 2000); H. Eakin, 'In
     Vienna, a New View of Wittgenstein Home', *New York Times* (28 August
     2003).

28 L. Wittgenstein, *Culture and Value* (Oxford, 1980), pp. 37e–38e.

29 'Architekturzentrum Wien', www.nextroom.at/building_article.
     php?building_id=2338&article_id=2967 (accessed June 2006). See also
     Leitner, *The Wittgenstein House*, for this reading.

30 See W. Wang, 'The Wittgenstein House – Review', *Architectural Review*
     (September 2001); P. Wijdeveld, *Ludwig Wittgenstein, Architect* (London,
     1994).

31 Letter to Margarete, September 1949; quoted in Wang, 'The
     Wittgenstein House'.

32 L. Wittgenstein, *Public and Private Occasions* (Lanham, MD, 2003), p. 25.

33 Ibid., pp. 33–4.

34 Monk, *Ludwig Wittgenstein*, p. 318.

35 Ibid., p. 339.

36 Ibid., p. 239.

37 Ibid., p. 314.

38 Wittgenstein, *Culture and Value*, pp. 18e–19e.

39 Ibid., p. 13e.

40 N. Malcolm, *Ludwig Wittgenstein: A Memoir* (Oxford, 2001), p. 35.

41 See Monk, *Ludwig Wittgenstein*, pp. 316–17.

42 McGuinness, *Young Ludwig*, pp. 48–9.

43 D. Stern, 'The Significance of Jewishness for Wittgenstein's Philosophy',
     Inquiry, XLIII (2000), p. 398. See also Stern, 'Was Wittgenstein a Jew?', in
     Wittgenstein: Biography and Philosophy, ed. J. Klagge (Cambridge, 2001).

6 Return to Cambridge and Philosophy, 1929–39

1 M. Brod, *Franz Kafka: A Biography* (New York, 1995), p. 98.

2 L. Wittgenstein, *Culture and Value* (Oxford, 1980), p. 6e.

3   Ibid., p. 56e.
4   M. Heidegger, *Introduction to Metaphysics* (New Haven, CT, and London, 2000), pp. 40–41.
5   M. Heidegger, *Being and Time* (Oxford, 1962), pp. 230–31.
6   Wittgenstein quoted in F. Waismann, *Wittgenstein and the Vienna Circle: Conversations* (Oxford, 1979), p. 68.
7   R. Monk, *Ludwig Wittgenstein: The Duty of Genius* (London, 1990), p. 271.
8   Wittgenstein, *Culture and Value*, p. 17e.
9   N. Malcolm, *Ludwig Wittgenstein: A Memoir* (Oxford, 2001), pp. 57–8.
10 Monk, *Ludwig Wittgenstein*, p. 256.
11 Both letters from 12 March 1933; *Ludwig Wittgenstein: Briefwechsel* (Innsbruck, 2004).
12 Monk, *Ludwig Wittgenstein*, p. 263.
13 Ibid., p. 262.
14 Ibid., p. 263.
15 M. Midgley, *The Owl of Minerva: A Memoir* (London, 2005).
16 K. T. Fann, ed., *Ludwig Wittgenstein: The Man and His Philosophy* (New York, 1967), p. 67.
17 L. Wittgenstein, 'Lecture on Ethics', in *Philosophical Occasions* (Indianapolis, IN, 1993), pp. 42ff.
18 B. Russell, *Autobiography* (London, 2000), p. 440.
19 Wittgenstein's exchanges with Turing are recorded in L. Wittgenstein, *Lectures on the Foundations of Mathematics, Cambridge, 1939* (Ithaca, NY, 1976).
20 V. Mehta, *Fly and the Fly-Bottle: Encounters with British Intellectuals* (Harmondsworth, 1965), p. 52.
21 Malcolm, *Ludwig Wittgenstein*, p. 25.
22 Ibid., p. 26.
23 Wittgenstein, *Culture and Value*, p. 57e.
24 L. Wittgenstein, *Public and Private Occasions* (Lanham, MD, 2003), p. 31.
25 F. Waismann, *Wittgenstein and the Vienna Circle: Conversations* (Oxford, 1979), p. 26.
26 Wittgenstein, *Philosophical Occasions*, p. 119.
27 Ibid., pp. 123, 125, 131.
28 Letter to Wittgenstein, 20 October 1933, in Wittgenstein, *Briefwechsel*.
29 Letter to Wittgenstein, 6 December 1936, in Wittgenstein, *Briefwechsel*.

30 Only one such encounter is mentioned, in MS 118, 22 September 1937.

31 MS 120, 2 December 1937.

32 See Monk, *Ludwig Wittgenstein*, Appendix.

33 MS 133, 26 October 1946.

34 Monk, *Ludwig Wittgenstein*, p. 427.

35 MS 125, 28 December 1941.

36 MS 133, 10 November 1946.

37 See Monk, *Ludwig Wittgenstein*, p. 342.

38 R. Rhees, ed., *Ludwig Wittgenstein: Personal Recollections* (Oxford, 1981), p. 35.

39 Wittgenstein, *Culture and Value*, p. 6e.

40 M. Heidegger, *Die Selbstbehauptung der deutschen Universität* (Frankfurt, 1982), p. 25.

41 One of his students, Casimir Lewy, is said to have described Wittgenstein as politically naïve.

42 Monk, *Ludwig Wittgenstein*, p. 353.

43 R. Rhees, ed., *Ludwig Wittgenstein: Personal Recollections* (Oxford, 1981), p. 158.

44 M. Amis, *Koba the Dread: Laughter and the Twenty Million* (London, 2002), p. 21.

45 See K. S. Johannessen, R. Larsen and K. O. Åmås, *Wittgenstein and Norway* (Oslo, 1994).

46 MS 183, 19 February 1937.

47 MS 120, 12 December 1937.

48 See L. Wittgenstein, *Lectures and Conversations on Aesthetics, Psychology and Religious Belief* (Oxford, 1966), on these lectures.

49 Wittgenstein, *Culture and Value*, p. 85e.

50 Wittgenstein, *Public and Private Occasions*, p. 211.

51 Wittgenstein, *Lectures and Conversations*, p. 56.

52 Wittgenstein, *Public and Private Occasions*, p. 203.

53 Wittgenstein, *Lectures and Conversations*, p. 70.

54 Wittgenstein, *Culture and Value*, p. 86e.

55 M. Drury, 'Conversations with Wittgenstein', in Rhees, *Ludwig Wittgenstein*, p. 79.

7 Professorship and Wartime, 1939–47

1   R. Monk, *Ludwig Wittgenstein: The Duty of Genius* (London, 1990), p. 343.

2   Ibid., p. 386.

3   MS 120, 14 March 1938. Wittgenstein was not actually a German citizen, since it was precisely the scope of the Nuremberg Laws to outstrip German Jews of their citizenship. He was what the Nazi law called a 'national', as opposed to a 'Reich citizen'.

4   MS 120, 16 March 1938.

5   Letter to Keynes, 18 March 1938; L. Wittgenstein, *Cambridge Letters*, ed. B. McGuiness and G. H. von Wright (Oxford, 1995).

6   Ambrose remained faithful to Wittgenstein's philosophy and published several other articles on Wittgenstein's philosophy of mathematics, which to this day present some of the most authoritative descriptions of his ideas on the subject. See A. Ambrose, *Essays in Analysis* (London, 1966).

7   R. Rhees, ed., *Ludwig Wittgenstein: Personal Recollections* (Oxford, 1981), p. 156.

8   Letter to Eccles, 27 March 1938; *Ludwig Wittgenstein: Briefwechsel* (Innsbruck, 2004).

9   L. Wittgenstein, *Lectures and Conversations on Aesthetics, Psychology and Religious Belief* (Oxford, 1966), p. 11, 17.

10 L. Wittgenstein, *Culture and Value* (Oxford 1980), p. 56e.

11 Wittgenstein, *Lectures and Conversations*, p. 8.

12 Monk, *Ludwig Wittgenstein*, p. 431.

13 Rhees, *Ludwig Wittgenstein*, p. 159.

14 Monk, *Ludwig Wittgenstein*, p. 433.

15 See Wittgenstein, *Lectures and Conversations*.

16 Ibid., p. 24.

17 Ibid., p. 51.

18 Ibid., p. 51.

19 Ibid., p. 43.

20 MS 133, 31 October 1946. It is true that around this time Wittgenstein also said that his own philosophy was akin to psychoanalysis. But the similarities should not be overstressed. See P. Hacker, 'Gordon Baker's Late Interpretation of Wittgenstein', in *Wittgenstein and His Interpreters*, ed. G. Kahane, E. Kanterian and O. Kuusela (Oxford, 2007). For more on

Wittgenstein on Freud, see J. Bouveresse, *Wittgenstein Reads Freud: The Myth of the Unconscious* (Princeton, NJ, 1995).

21 Helen Andrews to Ray Monk; see Monk, *Ludwig Wittgenstein*, pp. 449–50.
22 N. Bachtin, *Lectures and Essays* (Birmingham, 1963).
23 Rhees, *Ludwig Wittgenstein*, p. 28.
24 See his essay 'Aristotle versus Plato' in Bachtin, *Lectures and Essays*.
25 See T. Eagleton, 'Wittgenstein's Friends', *New Left Review*, 1/35 (1982).
26 L. Wittgenstein, *Lectures on the Foundations of Mathematics, Cambridge, 1939* (Ithaca, NY, 1976), p. 15.
27 Today the university hosts a Centre for Wittgensteinian Studies and edits a journal dedicated to the philosopher, *Philosophical Investigations*.
28 See also his *Remarks on the Philosophy of Psychology* and *Last Writings on the Philosophy of Psychology*, posthumously published in four volumes.
29 Letter to Malcolm, 15 December 1945.
30 Monk, *Ludwig Wittgenstein*, p. 463.
31 Ibid.
32 Letter to Malcolm, 20 September 1945; Wittgenstein, *Briefwechsel*.
33 B. McGuinness, *Approaches to Wittgenstein: Collected Papers* (London, 2002), p. 51.
34 Letter to Malcolm, around 20 August 1945.
35 Monk, *Ludwig Wittgenstein*, p. 480.
36 Wittgenstein, *Culture and Value*, pp. 48e–49e.
37 Currently, Wittgenstein's diary entries are the only source of information about the relationship. There are twenty letters from Richards to Wittgenstein deposited in the Austrian National Library, but they will not be accessible until 2020.
38 MS 131, 14 August 1946.
39 MS 130, 22 July 1946.
40 Rhees, *Ludwig Wittgenstein*, p. 162; Monk, *Ludwig Wittgenstein*, pp. 453–4.
41 MS 132, 30 September 1946.
42 N. Malcolm, *Ludwig Wittgenstein: A Memoir* (Oxford, 2001), p. 56.
43 O. P. Wood and G. Pitcher, eds, *Ryle* (London, 1970), p. 11.
44 Letter to Malcolm, 16 November 1947; Wittgenstein, *Briefwechsel*.

8 Nothing is Hidden: *Philosophical Investigations*

1 See I. Berlin, *Russian Thinkers* (London, 1979), pp. 22ff.
2 See P. Hacker, *Wittgenstein's Place in Twentieth Century Analytic Philosophy* (Oxford, 1996), pp. 98–9.
3 Another metaphor he employs is from the business world. He compares the philosopher to 'a chartered accountant [who] precisely investigates and clarifies the conduct of a business undertaking'. Like him the philosopher gives 'a complete survey of everything that may produce unclarity'; L. Wittgenstein, *Zettel*, ed. G.E.M. Anscombe and G. H. von Wright, trans. Anscombe (Oxford, 1967), §273.
4 D.A.T. Gasking and A. C. Jackson, 'Wittgenstein as a Teacher', in *Ludwig Wittgenstein: The Man and His Philosophy*, ed. K. T. Fann (New York, 1967), p. 51.
5 L. Wittgenstein, *Culture and Value* (Oxford 1980), p. 15e.
6 L. Wittgenstein, *Wittgenstein's Lectures: Cambridge, 1930–1932* (Oxford, 1980), pp. 21–2.
7 L. Wittgenstein, *The Big Typescript: TS 213* (Oxford, 2005), p. 304e.
8 L. Wittgenstein, *Public and Private Occasions* (Lanham, MD, 2003), p. 73.
9 There are many commentaries. Among the most reliable are P. Hacker, *Insight and Illusion* (Bristol, 1997); A. Kenny, *Wittgenstein* (Oxford, 2005); S. Schroeder, *Wittgenstein: The Way Out of the Fly-Bottle* (Cambridge, 2006).
10 Wittgenstein, *Culture and Value*, p. 14e.
11 Chapter II, 2.
12 Chapter IV.
13 'Iran's hard-line president on Saturday inaugurated a heavy-water production plant, a facility the West fears will be used to develop a nuclear bomb, as Tehran remained defiant ahead of a UN deadline that could lead to sanctions.' News headline on Yahoo.com on 26 August 2006, translated into Cockney using The Dialectizer on www.rinkworks.com/dialect/.
14 Wittgenstein, *The Big Typescript*, pp. 311e and 317e.

9 The Last Years, 1947–51

1 MS 137, 28 June 1948, 11 July 1948.
2 R. Monk, *Ludwig Wittgenstein: The Duty of Genius* (London, 1990), p. 525.
3 Ibid., p. 527.
4 MS 138, 25 February 1949.
5 Letter to Rhees, 31 August 1949. Gower is a peninsula near Swansea.
6 Monk, *Ludwig Wittgenstein*, p. 553.
7 Ibid., p. 558.
8 L. Wittgenstein, *On Certainty* (Oxford, 1996), §155.
9 O. K. Bouwsma, *Wittgenstein: Conversations, 1949–1951* (Indianapolis, IN, 1986), p. 60.
10 Ibid., p. 12.
11 N. Malcolm, *Ludwig Wittgenstein: A Memoir* (Oxford, 2001), p. 77.
12 Letter to Malcolm, end of November 1949; *Ludwig Wittgenstein: Briefwechsel* (Innsbruck, 2004).
13 Letter to Rhees, 7 May 1950; Wittgenstein, *Briefwechsel*.
14 L. Wittgenstein, *Culture and Value* (Oxford, 1980), pp. 83e–85e.
15 C. Wilson, *The Misfits: A Study of Sexual Outsiders* (London, 1988), p. 225.
16 Monk, *Ludwig Wittgenstein*, pp. 567–8.
17 Ibid., p. 573.
18 Wittgenstein was at times provided with issues of this magazine by Norman Malcolm, who sent them to Wittgenstein straight from America. He seems to have been an avid reader of this and other magazines since at least the early 1930s. Expressing his gratitude to Malcolm, Wittgenstein once wrote: 'Your mags are wonderful. How people can read *Mind* if they could read *Street & Smith* beats me. If philosophy has anything to do with wisdom there's certainly not a grain of that in *Mind*, and quite often a grain in the detective stories' (letter to Malcolm, 15 March 1948).
19 Wittgenstein, *On Certainty*, §532.

10 The Aftermath

1 P. F. Strawson, *Freedom and Resentment, and Other Essays* (London, 1974), p. 133.

2   A. Kenny, *Wittgenstein* (Oxford, 2005), p. xii.

3   R. Monk, *Ludwig Wittgenstein: The Duty of Genius* (London 1990), p. 486.

4   L. Wittgenstein, *Culture and Value* (Oxford, 1980), p. 66e.

5   For two conflicting views on this issue, see G. H. von Wright, *The Tree of Knowledge and Other Essays* (Leiden, 1993), and H.-J. Glock, 'Was Wittgenstein an Analytic Philosopher?', *Metaphilosophy*, xxxv/4 (2004).

6   See R. Monk, *Ludwig Wittgenstein: The Duty of Genius* (London 1990), p. 466.

7   B. McGuinness, *Young Ludwig: Wittgenstein's Life, 1889–1921* (Oxford, 2005), p. 100.

8   R. Rhees, ed., *Recollections of Wittgenstein* (Oxford, 1984), pp. 125–6.

9   P. Hacker, 'Wittgenstein, Ludwig Josef Johann (1889–1951)', *Oxford Dictionary of National Biography* (Oxford, 2004).

10 Wittgenstein, *Culture and Value*, p. 46e.

Bibliography

Cited writings by Ludwig Wittgenstein

'Lecture on Ethics', in *Philosophical Occasions*
Lectures and Conversations on Aesthetics, Psychology and Religious Belief (Oxford, 1966)
Zettel, ed. G.E.M. Anscombe and G. H. von Wright, trans. Anscombe (Oxford, 1967)
Lectures on the Foundations of Mathematics, Cambridge, 1939 (Ithaca, NY, 1976)
Culture and Value (Oxford, 1980)
Wittgenstein's Lectures. Cambridge, 1930–1932 (Oxford, 1980)
Philosophical Occasions (Indianapolis, IN, 1993)
On Certainty (Oxford, 1996)
Cambridge Letters (Oxford, 1997)
Philosophical Investigations (Oxford, 1998) [here abbreviated as 'PI']
Wittgenstein's Nachlass: The Bergen Electronic Edition (Bergen and Oxford, 2000) [references to Wittgenstein's MSS follow this edition]
Tractatus Logico-Philosophicus (London, 2001)
Public and Private Occasions (Lanham, MD, 2003)
Ludwig Wittgenstein: Briefwechsel (Innsbruck, 2004)
The Big Typescript: TS 213 (Oxford, 2005)

Secondary literature

'Architekturzentrum Wien',
www.nextroom.at/building_article.php?building_id=2338&article_id=2967 (accessed June 2006)
Ambrose, A., *Essays in Analysis* (London, 1966)

—, and M. Lazerowitz, eds, *Ludwig Wittgenstein: Philosophy and Language* (London, 1972)

Amis, M., *Koba the Dread: Laughter and the Twenty Million* (London, 2002)

Anscombe, E., and P. Geach, *Three Philosophers* (Oxford, 1967)

Bachtin, N., *Lectures and Essays* (Birmingham, 1963)

Baker, G., and P. Hacker, *An Analytical Commentary on the Philosophical Investigations*, 4 vols (Oxford, 1980–96)

Bartley, W. W., *Wittgenstein*, III (La Salle, IL, 1986)

Berlin, I., *Russian Thinkers* (London, 1979)

Bouveresse, J., *Wittgenstein Reads Freud: The Myth of the Unconscious* (Princeton, NJ, 1995)

Bouwsma, O. K., *Wittgenstein: Conversations, 1949–1951* (Indianapolis, IN, 1986)

Brod, M., *Franz Kafka: A Biography* (New York, 1995)

Cornish, K., *The Jew of Linz* (London, 1998)

Drury, M., 'Conversations with Wittgenstein', in *Ludwig Wittgenstein: Personal Recollections*, ed. R. Rhees (Oxford, 1981)

Eagleton, T., 'Wittgenstein's Friends', *New Left Review*, I/35 (1982)

—, 'Introduction to Wittgenstein', in *Wittgenstein: The Terry Eagleton Script; The Derek Jarman Film* (Worcester, MA, 1993)

Eakin, H., 'In Vienna, a New View of Wittgenstein Home', *New York Times*, 28 August 2003

Engelmann, P., *Letters from Ludwig Wittgenstein with a Memoir* (Oxford, 1967)

Fann, K. T., ed., *Ludwig Wittgenstein: The Man and His Philosophy* (New York, 1967)

Gasking, D.A.T., and A. C. Jackson, 'Wittgenstein as a Teacher', in *Ludwig Wittgenstein: The Man and His Philosophy*, ed. K. T. Fann (New York 1967)

Glock, H.-J., *A Wittgenstein Dictionary* (Oxford, 1996)

—, 'Was Wittgenstein an Analytic Philosopher?', *Metaphilosophy*, XXXV/4 (2004)

Hacker, P., *Wittgenstein's Place in Twentieth Century Analytic Philosophy* (Oxford, 1996)

—, *Insight and Illusion* (Bristol, 1997)

—, 'Wittgenstein, Ludwig Josef Johann (1889–1951)', *Oxford Dictionary of National Biography* (Oxford, 2004)

—, 'Gordon Baker's Late Interpretation of Wittgenstein', in *Wittgenstein and His Interpreters*, ed. G. Kahane, E. Kanterian and O. Kuusela (forthcoming)

Hamann, B., *Hitler's Vienna: A Dictator's Apprenticeship* (Oxford, 1999)

Hargrove, E. C., 'Wittgenstein, Bartley, and the Glöckel School Reform',
    Journal of the History of Philosophy, XVIII (1980)

Heidegger, M., *Being and Time* (Oxford, 1962)

—, *Die Selbstbehauptung der deutschen Universität* (Frankfurt, 1982)

—, *Introduction to Metaphysics* (New Haven, CT, 2000)

Hertz, H. R., *The Principles of Mechanics* (London, 1899)

Hintikka, J., *On Wittgenstein* (Belmont, CA, 2000)

Janik, A., and S. Toulmin, *Wittgenstein's Vienna* (New York, 1973)

Johannessen, K. S., R. Larsen and K. O. Åmås, *Wittgenstein and Norway* (Oslo,
    1994)

Kahane, G., E. Kanterian and O. Kuusela, eds, *Wittgenstein and His Interpreters*
    (forthcoming)

Kenny, A., *Wittgenstein* (Oxford, 2005)

Klagge, J., ed., *Wittgenstein: Biography and Philosophy* (Cambridge, 2001)

Leitner, B., *The Wittgenstein House* (New York, 2000)

Liiceanu, G., *The Paltinis Diary* (Budapest, 2000)

McGuinness, B., *Approaches to Wittgenstein: Collected Papers* (London, 2002)

—, *Young Ludwig: Wittgenstein's Life, 1889–1921* (Oxford, 2005)

Malcolm, N., *A Religious Point of View?* (London, 1993)

—, *Ludwig Wittgenstein: A Memoir* (Oxford, 2001)

Mehta, V., *Fly and the Fly-Bottle: Encounters with British Intellectuals*
    (Harmondsworth, 1965)

Midgley, M., *The Owl of Minerva: A Memoir* (London, 2005)

Monk, R., *Ludwig Wittgenstein: The Duty of Genius* (London, 1990)

Nedo, M., and M. Ranchetti, *Wittgenstein: Sein Leben in Bildern und Texten*
    (Frankfurt, 1983)

Pascal, F., 'Wittgenstein: A Personal Memoir', in *Ludwig Wittgenstein: Personal
    Recollections*, ed. R. Rhees (Oxford, 1981)

Pears, D., *The False Prison: A Study of the Development of Wittgenstein's
    Philosophy* (Oxford, 1987–8)

Perloff, M., *Wittgenstein's Ladder: Poetic Language and the Strangeness of the
    Ordinary* (Chicago, IL, 1996)

Redpath, T., *Wittgenstein: A Student's Memoir* (London, 1990)

Rhees, R., ed., *Ludwig Wittgenstein: Personal Recollections* (Oxford, 1981)

—, *Recollections of Wittgenstein* (Oxford, 1984)

Rozema, D., '*Tractatus Logico-Philosophicus*: A "Poem" by Ludwig

Wittgenstein', *Journal of the History of Ideas*, LXIII/2 (2002)

Russell, B., *Autobiography* (London, 2000)

Sarnitz, A., *Adolf Loos* (London, 2003)

Schroeder, S., *Wittgenstein: The Way out of the Fly-Bottle* (Cambridge, 2006)

Stern, D., 'The Significance of Jewishness for Wittgenstein's Philosophy',
    Inquiry, XLIII (2000)

—, 'Was Wittgenstein a Jew?', in *Wittgenstein: Biography and Philosophy*,
    ed. J. Klagge (Cambridge, 2001)

Strawson, P. F., *Freedom and Resentment, and Other Essays* (London, 1974)

Timms, E., *Karl Kraus: Apocalyptic Satirist: Culture and Catastrophe in Habsburg
    Vienna* (New Haven, CT, and London 1986)

Waismann, F., *Wittgenstein and the Vienna Circle: Conversations* (Oxford, 1979)

—, *The Principles of Linguistic Philosophy* (Basingstoke, 1997)

Wall, R., *Wittgenstein in Ireland* (London, 2000)

Wang, W., 'The Wittgenstein House – Review', *Architectural Review*
    (September 2001)

Weininger, O., *Sex and Character* (London, 1906)

Weinzierl, U., 'Der Fluch des Hauses Wittgenstein', *Die Welt*, 5 July 2003

Wijdeveld, P., *Ludwig Wittgenstein, Architect* (London, 1994)

Wilson, C., *The Misfits: A Study of Sexual Outsiders* (London, 1988)

Wittgenstein, H., 'Recollections' (1948), unpublished

—, 'My Brother Ludwig', in *Ludwig Wittgenstein: Personal Recollections*,
    ed. R. Rhees (Oxford, 1981)

Wood, O. P., and G. Pitcher, eds, *Ryle* (London, 1970)

Wright, G. H. von, *The Tree of Knowledge and Other Essays* (Leiden, 1993)

Websites

www.nextroom.at (Haus Wittgenstein)

www.spiluttini.com (Haus Wittgenstein)

gandalf.aksis.uib.no/wab/ (Wittgenstein Archives in Bergen)

plato.stanford.edu/entries/wittgenstein/

www.uweb.ucsb.edu/~luke_manning/tractatus/tractatus–jsnav.html
    (*Tractatus* online)

www.marxists.org/reference/subject/philosophy/works/at/wittgens.htm
    (Wittgenstein's lectures on philosophy, 1932–3)

Acknowledgements

I would like to thank Ame Berges, Jakob A. Bertzbach, Anna Dimitrijevics, Peter Hacker, Steven Hall, Guy Kahane, Michael Stoynov and Ivaylo Vlaev for suggestions and discussions. Gustav Klimt's painting of Wittgenstein's sister (p. 18) can be found in the Neue Pinakothek, Munich; the photograph on page 188 comes from the Library of Congress, Washington, DC (Prints and Photographs Division), and the opening page of the 'Wittgenstein Motet' is reproduced by kind permission of Schott Music Limited, London (p. 202; all rights reserved).